Things Made and Things Said
Teachers, Pupils and the Craft of Writing

Things Made and Things Said
Teachers, Pupils and the Craft of Writing

Gertrude Patterson

With contributions from teachers and pupils
from schools from the North and South of Ireland
and a chapter
by
CLARE MALONEY

Foreword by Brendan Kennelly

Belfast
The Stranmillis Press

First published in 1999 by
The Stranmillis Press
(an imprint of
Stranmillis University College,
Belfast BT9 5DY)
www.stran-ni.ac.uk

British Library Cataloguing in Publication Data
A catalogue record for this book is available from the
British Library

ISBN 0903009285

Designed by Cilla Wagner and set in 12 on 13.5pt Garamond

Printed digitally by Textflow Services Limited, Belfast.
E-mail: enq@textflow.nireland.com
Telephone: 01232 660868
Fax: 01232 660241

CONTENTS

Foreword   Brendan Kennelly   vii

Acknowledgements   ix

Introduction   1

Chapter One
          'Words alone are certain good'   7

Chapter Two
          'That poetry is made with words'   41

Chapter Three
          'In the saying and the doing'
          Clare Maloney   77

Poems   115

Bibliography   163

Notes on the Authors   173

FOREWORD

Now and then one comes across a book which strikes one as having been written out of decades of experience, of calm, intense meditation on that experience, and of an ability to structure and express that meditation in such a way that the reader is convinced that he/she is in the presence of wisdom. Not many books today even begin to be interested in this kind of wisdom, this lucid, concentrated, elegant expression and sharing of almost a lifetime's experience. But Gertrude Patterson is interested in writing this kind of book. In my view, she has succeeded brilliantly.

Three things have always struck me about Gertrude Patterson. The first is that she is an excellent critic. Her work on T. S. Eliot is as fresh, erudite and perceptive to-day as when she first published her book on his poetry. She has written equally well on Philip Larkin and Seamus Heaney; and her interest in modern poetry extends well beyond the work of these writers. In fact, her interest has deepened to such an extent that, as this book shows, she is now a deeply philosophical critic brooding on the nature and consequences of poetry, the writing of it, the reading of it, the discussion, analysing and remembering of it. As her philosophy deepens, her style becomes more and more determined to open itself to all kinds of voices – the voices of many and varied poets, of critics, of teachers and students who get involved with poetry and the language that is its body and soul. I hesitated to use that word 'philosophical', thinking it might imply that I consider Dr Patterson's writing to be so complex and dense as to be almost impenetrable; it's the opposite of that; it's clear and concentrated at once, always stimulating and illuminating. It has a feeling of newness about it; it's as if she'd taken Ezra Pound's "Make it new" very much to heart. As readers will soon discover, Gertrude Patterson has indeed made it new.

The second thing about her is that she's a hardworking, shrewd, experimental, open-hearted and tough-minded teacher. Only a teacher with these qualities could have written this book which is, among other things, a delightful anthology of poems by students and teachers alike. Gertrude Patterson is the sort of teacher who never stops learning; she knows that her students teach her as much as she teaches her students; and all that knowledge is there to be shared by everybody in the classroom.

Thirdly, she is a sharp, compassionate listener. This ability to listen in such a manner implies a special kind of critical respect for what the other is trying to say. She brings this capacity for acute, sustained, respectful, critical listening to bear not only on students and other teachers, but on poetry itself. She listens to poems as people sometimes listen to heartbeats. She puts her ear to the living being of people and of poetry.

Things Made and Things Said is of real value to students, teachers, writers, those planning and working to be writers, critics, readers of various kinds. It is a sensible, substantial, enthusiastic book dealing clearly with complex matters. It is an extremely humane book; the truth that people write poems for themselves and for other people is never lost sight of here. The book is utterly unpretentious, devoid of critical smartalecry or gimmicry. It is full of surprises, a joy to read. Better still is the thrill of re-reading it. That's when the book's calm, deep wisdom really establishes itself.

Brendan Kennelly
Professor of Modern Literature
Trinity College Dublin

ACKNOWLEDGEMENTS

I am very grateful to all those who have contributed to this publication: first, to the officers and staff of the South Eastern Education and Library Board for inviting me to contribute to their in-service programme of courses for language co-ordinators and to the many teachers who took part in those courses. I am particularly indebted to Mr Tom Morwood, former Primary Adviser for the South Eastern Education and Library Board, and to Mrs Muriel Stringer, a former Field Officer for English, for all their help and support in organising the programme. During these courses and others which I conducted in various Teachers' Centres for the North Eastern Board, I had the opportunity to meet teachers from a wide variety of schools and it was a great privilege as a result to have been invited to teach poetry to their pupils and to have further meetings with their staff. I am indebted to the principals of the schools involved for the warmth of their welcome as I am to the teachers and pupils who went on to write their own poems, many of which are included in this collection. I am also grateful to Professor Alex McEwen and the School of Education in The Queen's University, Belfast, for inviting me to contribute to their Master's degree programme by establishing a new course in this important area of the curriculum. The teachers who took the module on poetry as part of their degree study worked very hard to write poetry themselves and I am grateful to them. In particular, I must thank Clare Maloney, a former teacher from County Louth, who has worked closely with me, first, in the preparation of her MEd thesis and currently in undertaking further research in this area for her PhD. She has made a significant contribution to the book, despite a busy work schedule writing curriculum materials for schools in the Republic of Ireland. Her enthusiasm for writing has been a constant source of motivation and inspiration to me, extending my research for the book to include schools — and hence a wider community of writers – in the south of Ireland, and enabling me in the process to be much better informed about curriculum innovations taking place there. Though it was not the original intention of the publication to be a venture in North-South relationships, the fact that it has achieved much in this direction is due, in no small part, to Clare herself.

I am very conscious that the book is itself 'a thing made' as well as a 'thing said' and acknowledge here the number of colleagues in Stranmillis University College who have been involved in its publication : Ron Barron, former Head of Learning Resources, the staff of Information Technology Services and the Library, always prepared to give generously of their time and help, much of it often beyond the call of duty. I am also most grateful to Barbara Ellison, Head of Art and Design, who made the suggestion of using a print of an early Irish patchwork quilt for the cover, and to the curator of the Down County Museum for permission to use it. Special tribute must be made to Wesley McCann, Librarian, and Cilla Wagner, Head and Manager of the Learning Support Services respectively, who took such care in preparing the manuscript for publication. Combined with Cilla Wagner's sense of design, Wesley McCann's love of books as objects of art in themselves, his knowledge of print and printing, his meticulous attention to detail, and the enthusiastic professionalism which he has applied in ensuring that the book is a thing 'well made', as Yeats might have put it, have made the preparation of it a personal as well as a professional pleasure.

I would like to thank the Principal, Professor Richard McMinn, for his support in the publication of the book and the former Principal, Dr Robert Rodgers, for enabling me to pursue my work for the Education and Library Boards in the various projects in which I have been involved. I also appreciate the encouragement and support of Sam Burnside of the Verbal Arts Centre in Londonderry, Her Grace The Duchess of Abercorn and Ann McKay of the Pushkin Prizes Trust, Eleanor Houston, Peter Frost and my colleagues in the English Department, always ready to be patient listeners and counsellors. Special thanks must go to Brendan Kennelly, Professor of Modern Literature, Trinity College, Dublin, poet, teacher, scholar and friend, for his enormous generosity in writing the Foreword.

The publication of this book is testimony to the collaborative partnerships which the College has maintained with teachers and former students over the years, through its pre-service and in-service provision, and the willingness of school principals to co-operate in so many aspects of our college functions. A great many schools produced poetry and I must apologise if there are any omissions from the list which follows or indeed if I have mistakenly attributed a poem to the wrong forename. A project which has spanned many years makes it almost inevitable that something will go astray. Though not all of the staff and pupils who participated will be explicitly represented in the pages which follow, I can assure all of the schools and colleges listed here that I am most grateful for their help, for each of them contributed in some way to the making of this book.

Annahilt Primary School, Hillsborough, Co. Down
Ballymacash Primary School, Lisburn, Co. Antrim
Ballymacward Primary School, Lisburn, Co. Antrim
Ballyoran Primary School, Portadown, Co. Armagh
Banbridge High School, Banbridge, Co. Down
Bangor Central Primary School, Bangor, Co. Down
Belfast Royal Academy, Belfast
Belvoir Primary School, Belfast
Ben Madigan Preparatory School, Belfast
Bloomfield Road Primary School, Bangor, Co. Down
Brooklands Primary School, Belfast
Cairnshill Primary School, Belfast
Castle Gardens Primary School, Newtownards, Co. Down
Clandeboye Primary School, Bangor, Co. Down
Convent of Mercy Primary School, Downpatrick, Co. Down
Comber Primary School, Comber, Co. Down
Donaghadee Primary School, Donaghadee, Co. Down
Dundonald Primary School, Dundonald, Belfast
Dunmurry Primary School, Dunmurry, Co. Antrim
Good Shepherd Primary School, Belfast
Grange Park Primary School, Bangor, Co. Down

Harding Memorial Primary School, Belfast
Harmony Hill Primary School, Lisburn, Co. Antrim
Holy Family Girls' Primary School, Belfast
Holywood Primary School, Holywood, Co. Down
Kilcooley Primary School, Bangor, Co. Down
Kilmaine Primary School, Bangor, Co. Down
King's Park Primary School, Lurgan, Co. Armagh
Knockmore Primary School, Lisburn, Co. Antrim
Largymore Primary School, Lisburn, Co. Antrim
Lisburn Central Primary School, Lisburn, Co. Armagh
Lurgan College of Further Education, Lurgan, Co. Armagh
Model Girls' Secondary School, Belfast
Moira Primary School, Moira, Co. Antrim
Mossley Primary School, Newtownabbey, Co. Antrim
North Down College of Further Education, Bangor, Co. Down
Portadown College of Further Education, Portadown, Co. Armagh
Regent House School, Newtownards, Co. Down
Sacred Heart Primary School, Lurgan, Co. Armagh
Seymour Hill Primary School, Dunmurry, Co. Antrim
St Aloysius Primary School, Belfast
St Anthony's Primary School, Craigavon, Co. Armagh
St Bride's Primary School, Belfast
St Brigid's Primary School, Downpartick, Co. Down
St Catherine's Convent Primary School, Belfast
St Finian's Primary School, Newtownards, Co. Down
St Gall's Primary School, Belfast
St John's Primary School, Gilford, Co. Armagh
St Joseph's Primary School, Ballymena, Co. Antrim
St Joseph's Primary School, Carryduff, Belfast
St Kevin's Primary School, Belfast
St Kieran's Primary School, Belfast
St Luke's Primary School, Lisburn, Co. Antrim
St Malachy's Primary School, Bangor, Co. Down
St Mark's Primary School, Dunmurry, Co. Antrim
St Mary's University College, Belfast
St Mary's Primary School, Newcastle, Co. Down

St Mary's Primary School, Newtownards, Co. Down
St Mary's Primary School, Portaferry, Co. Down
St Peter's Primary School, Belfast
St Teresa's Boys' Primary School, Belfast
Stabannon Primary School, Co. Louth
The Dominican College, Belfast
The Model Boys' Secondary School, Belfast
Tonagh Primary School, Lisburn, Co. Armagh
Tower View Primary School, Bangor, Co. Down
Waringstown Primary School, Craigavon, Co. Armagh
Wellington College, Belfast
Whitehouse Primary School, Newtownabbey, Co. Antrim

... and the pupils of schools at both Primary and Secondary level – which unfortunately cannot be listed separately here – who took part in the Children's Workshop, 'A Ladder to the Moon', held in the Irish Writers' Centre, Parnell Square, Dublin, 25-29 July, 1994.

Gertrude Patterson

INTRODUCTION

The idea for this book and the concept of the teaching and writing of poetry which underlies it have their origins in a deeply-held personal conviction that there must be a correlation between the ways in which poets learn the practice of their art and the methods which teachers might use to encourage and promote the skills of writing in the classroom. Some years ago, when I was writing a book on the poetry of T. S. Eliot and teaching in a school at the same time, the validity of this notion became particularly apparent to me. Eliot was working at a time of experimentation in all the arts, when learning new ways of recording experience was at the forefront of the minds of all those who were engaged in writing, whatever form it took. In 1908, a Poets' Club was formed in London by the then comparatively unknown T. E. Hulme, and from the moment of its first meeting, there began the earliest attempts in England to emancipate poetry from what was perceived by the participants to be the devitalised forms and idioms which characterised the poetry of his time. Hulme called for a new 'classicism': an approach to poetry which demanded a recognition from poets that they were not angels speaking to men of things beyond the scope of ordinary comprehension – which characterised, for Hulme, the romantic view of the artist – but *craftsmen,* with the ability to record observations and perceptions accurately and succinctly.[1] For Hulme, as for the Imagist movement in poetry which he founded, such observation and the accurate language in which it was recorded, crystallised in the Image.

It was the discussions of the group and the Manifesto to which they all assented, which seemed to me to offer teachers much better guidance on the skills of writing than any publication on the teaching and writing of poetry with which I, a young teacher myself, was familiar. To begin with, they all agreed that writing poetry was not a matter of sudden inspiration and illumination, but hard work! This contrasted in quite a dramatic way with the dewy-eyed view of educationalists like Sybil Marshall[2] and others in the period of the Sixties when I started to teach, who claimed that children simply loved to write and that the only challenge facing the teacher was to provide the right stimulus to enable it to take place. In contrast, for Hulme, as for all the Imagists, the task for the poet was a struggle to master his medium: less a matter of having something important to say than to find the most effective and accurate means of conveying meaning. Extracts from the writing of some of the Imagists show the extent to which Hulme's teaching was taken seriously. F. S. Flint, for example, who wrote 'The History of Imagism', declared his 'rules' for good writing:

1.   Direct treatment of the thing whether subjective or objective.
2.   To use absolutely no word that did not contribute to the presentation.
3.   As regarding rhythm: to compose in the sequence of the musical phrase, not in the sequence of the metronome.[3]

And here is a similar policy statement, this time from Ezra Pound, who contributed to the famous Imagist Manifesto when he joined the group:

1.   To use the language of common speech, but to employ always the exact word, not the nearly exact, nor merely the decorative word.

             .   .   .   .

4.   To present the image (hence the name: "Imagist"). We are not a school of painters, but we believe that poetry should render particulars exactly and not deal in vague generalities, however magnificent and sonorous. It is for this reason that we oppose the cosmic poet, who seems to shirk the real difficulties of his art.
5.   To produce poetry which is hard and clear, never blurred or indefinite.
6.   Finally, most of us believe that concentration is of the essence in poetry.[4]

To teach children the value of the image in the interest of accuracy rather than, as popularly supposed, as 'decorative' language to 'dress up' ordinary speech in the appropriate garb of poetry, seems to me to have been one of the best lessons to have been learned from the Imagists.

T. S. Eliot was not himself a member of Hulme's Poets' Club, but he came to know of its ideas from his long association with Ezra Pound, an American expatriate like himself, who acted as a mentor and teacher of many of the poets of his day, including W. B. Yeats, instructing and guiding them on how to make their work more 'accurate' in the Hulme sense of the term. His revision of Eliot's great poem, *The Waste Land*, or what came to be know as his 'Caesarian' role, is well documented, a process carried out in his famous blue pencil with none of the tact of the sensitive English teacher, which cut the first version of the manuscript to less than half of its original length. Examining the manuscripts of *The Waste Land* where they are held in the Berg Collection of the New York Public Library shortly before the publication of my book, taught me a great deal about the craft of writing. Like the draft versions of other poets' work, they indicated the enormous efforts which have to be made by real craftsmen to state exactly what they mean. The prose work of T. S. Eliot and Ezra Pound on the art of writing, together with their correspondence and the advice and comment which Pound provided during the drafting and editing processes of *The Waste Land*, tell us much about how poets learn from one another. What they teach, above all, is that writing poetry is initially a craft which has to be learned and practised: poems are rarely the result of sudden inspiration, written in one session, which is how pupils are so often expected to produce them in the classroom.

In the light of all this experience it was of great interest to me to read in Professor Cox's Report – on which the National Curriculum for England and Wales is based (echoing, too, the earlier Kingman Report) – comment which seemed to endorse these views:

Good Primary teachers pay attention to the process of writing, developed from knowledge and understanding of the practice of real writers (including themselves); they are then able to provide classroom practices which allow children to behave like real writers.[5]

The emphasis which Cox places here on the knowledge of how experienced writers work and the need for teachers to be involved in the writing processes themselves, are of the utmost importance if teachers are to break down some of the prejudices against poetry writing prevalent in many schools, where it is treated, as Bullock had earlier pointed out in *A Language for Life,* as something 'precious, arcane, to be revered', 'something more or less   involuntarily secreted by the author', 'oozing from the unconscious in a manner quite unlike that of prose'.[6] In statements such as Professor Cox's, implicit also in the Report of the English Working Party for Northern Ireland, there seems to be something of the new period of 'classicism' which Hulme demanded, replacing in our schools some of the more romantic and idealistic notions of the 'creative' and 'free' writing of the Sixties. Such approaches, underscored by an emphasis on the place of drafting and editing advocated by our present curriculum for English, certainly lead teachers away from the notion of poetry as an inaccessible form of utterance and the creative act as a single spontaneous verbal gesture.

In putting some of these ideas to the test, I am grateful to the teachers and pupils who have contributed either directly or indirectly to the writing of this book. Work for it started a number of years ago when I was invited by the South Eastern Education and Library Board to contribute to their programme of courses for the Language Co-ordinators in their schools, designed to help them to implement the recommendations of the *Primary Language and Literacy Guidelines* for Northern Ireland. All acknowledged their reluctance to teach poetry and therefore a particular need in this important area of the curriculum. As a result of these courses and the friendships I made, I was privileged to have been invited to teach in many of the schools in which these teachers worked. Many of the poems in the book are a direct result of those sessions. Later, I had the opportunity to contribute a module, *Approaches to Poetry – Process and Product,* as part of the Master in Education programme of the School of Education in Queen's University, Belfast. During this course, teachers were encouraged (they would say, compelled!) to write poetry themselves, partly to gain knowledge and understanding of the writing process, but also that they might be better able to write alongside their pupil apprentices. Most of the teachers' poems included in the book have their origins in this course.

The work of all those who contributed to this book will certainly testify to the fact that poetry writing is not easy, but that in the processes of doing it and in learning from one another, as well as from the work of more experienced poets, they have felt themselves to be part of a community of writers. The chapter written by Clare Maloney, a former teacher from a small village school near Drogheda, makes this particularly clear. Initially, with no specialised knowledge and no overwhelming enthusiasm for English, she came to writing as a real novice, so that she had no difficulty in identifying her own 'raids on the inarticulate', as Eliot would have described them, with the efforts of her pupils and the 'real' poets whose work she has studied. Insisting, along with the many young poets whose work is included in this book, that poetry is made with words, she, like them, is affirming that the sense of community which all discover in the creative process, is one which does not have to rely on a sense of a shared political, religious or any other ideology to identify its common purpose, but on what Ezra Pound called 'an unending adventure' towards 'arrangement' in the things-made and things-said of the completed poem.

1   T. E. Hulme, 'Romanticism and Classicism', *Speculations: Essays on Humanism and Philosophy of Art* , edited by Herbert read (Lon don: K. Paul, Trench, Trubner, 1924).

2   Sibil Marshall, *An Experiment in Education,* (Cambridge: Cam bridge University Press, 1963), is a typical example.

3   from *Poetry,* March 1913, reprinted in *Imagist Poetry,* edited by Peter Jones (Harmondsworth: Penguin,1972), p.18.

4   Preface to *Some Imagist Poets* 1915, reprinted in *Imagist Poetry*, p.135.

5   *English for ages 5 to 11* [the first Cox Report]. Department of Education and Science (London: DES, 1988), Chapter 2.11, p.8.

6   *A Language for Life* [the Bullock Report]. Report of the Committee of Inquiry appointed by the Secretary of State for Education and Science (London: HMSO, 1975), 9.22.

CHAPTER ONE

'Words alone are certain good'

Poetry, Cultural Heritage
and
the Northern Ireland Curriculum

IN ARISTOPHANES'S PLAY, *THE FROGS*, the question is asked, 'What do you want the poet for?', and the answer given, 'To save the city, of course', an indication of the privileged place which poetry held in ancient Greece and of the kind of wisdom which was expected from poets at times of national crisis – in the situation of *The Frogs*, the threat of destruction itself in the Peloponnesian War. To-day, poets occupy a more modest place; indeed few would want to be brought in to cope with the sorts of national disasters that face the modern world, unlike the poet, Seanachan, in Yeats's play, *The King's Threshold*, who goes on hunger strike and is prepared to die rather than give up his place on the king's council. In cultures where national prosperity is measured in terms of productivity by commercial and utilitarian means, it would be hard to quantify the values of art and literature in the accumulated wisdom of the race as part of the gross national product on an export/import axis. 'Education for Life' is the key concept which is offered to all of us charged with the education of teachers and hence with responsibility for the pupils they go on to teach, but the 'life' for which they are to be prepared, we are constantly told, is less the inner world of the spirit than the world of work: a world of *doing* rather than of *being*. T. E. Hulme, the eminent aesthetician who had such an important influence on the great poetry of the beginning of this century, put it well in another context, in his essay 'Bergson's Theory of Art':

Man's primary need is not *knowledge* but *action*. . . . The function of the intellect is so to present things not that we may most thoroughly understand them, but that we may successfully act on them.[1]

Faced then with the challenges of the compulsions to provide within the educational system adequate preparation for our pupils to enable them to acquire the skills of *doing* rather than *thinking* and *knowing*, what is the place of literature in general and of poetry in particular in the school curriculum? The Northern Ireland Curriculum confidently asserts that 'poetry needs to be at the heart of work in English because of the quality of language at work on experience it offers us.'[2] But what is that language, and why is it so desirable that our pupils acquire an appreciation of it so that they can gain access to it themselves? In 1963, the Newsom Report, *Half Our Future*, cautioned that poetry should not be regarded as a 'minor amenity' in the English curriculum for secondary schools but a 'major channel of experience'.[3] How can we make it so? How can it be a major channel in helping to prepare our pupils, not only for the world of work, but to cope with the personal challenges which they meet, particularly in the divided society of Northern Ireland? Should poetry be perceived as a potent instrument in developing social awareness and hence social change, as Bullock suggested had been the aim of some teachers in the Sixties, where literature was used – usually in the form of 'filleted extracts' from texts on a common theme – in order to stimulate discussion on social issues in the classroom? For such teachers, as Bullock saw it, the traditional notion of 'bridging the social gap' by sharing the values of a common culture is unacceptable, not only because, for them, it fails to work but because it implies the superiority of a 'middle class culture'.[4] Is the place of poetry in the curriculum then simply an attempt to preserve and transmit the values of our cultural heritage as they are embodied in the 'best' writers from the classics in the great tradition of English or Anglo-Irish literature? The foremost poet of our own century, T. S. Eliot, claimed that any attempt to describe the nature and value of poetry in terms of 'the inculcation of morals, or the direction of politics' or 'religion or an equivalent of religion' was a 'monstrous abuse of words'.[5] In going on, however, to describe it as a 'superior amusement . . . *pour distraire les honnêtes gens*,'[6] he is not relegating it to the minor channel of experience that Newsom referred to but rather attempting to avoid making unrealistic claims for its 'usefulness' as a 'criticism of life' – as the critic F. R. Leavis was later to do, arguing the centrality of litera-ture in maintaining the moral welfare of the nation.[7] It would have to be added however, that the approaches to teaching and determin-ing a literary hierarchy advocated by Leavis had nothing in common with those of the socially concerned groups of the Sixties for whom literature was judged, in Bullock's terms, purely for its 'social yield'.[8] How then should those of us concerned with education to-day an-swer Aristophanes's question? If not to save the city, what do we want the poet for?

Northern Ireland has for too long been the victim of its own par-tial knowledge of its past: a blinkered and edited vision of history and the opposing cultural traditions in which the selected events and the personages associated with them are enshrined, which has impris-oned us in a darkness of mind, compelling too many of us to violent action rather than providing us with the illumination of true knowl-edge and understanding from which a real future might be built. We trust that we may be emerging from that darkness, and one of the major obligations of what has come to be known as the 'peace proc-ess', however falteringly it has taken place, is to educate our young people in a new understanding of themselves, their history and their identity, whether it be of Protestant Ulsterman, Catholic Irishman or Citizen of Europe. For all of us involved in teaching at whatever level, the question of what we want the poet for has assumed a very particular sense of urgency over the past thirty years and more, on both sides of the political divide, north and south of the border. Often teachers are asked what they are doing to prepare our pupils for the environment they currently inhabit, quite apart from the unknown world of the future, and what the 'relevance' of literature is to either of these. Over the years, I have often had cause to wonder myself, sitting in a tutorial room with a group of students, talking about image in the poetry of Yeats or Larkin, while not so far away from the safe world of the college, terrorists have been plotting destruction and political havoc; the whole thing brought that much nearer to us all when this same world of teaching and learning is juxtaposed with the real world of action and suffering from which the literature we are teaching springs and to which our learners as young teachers themselves have to return to work in the classrooms of east and west Belfast, east and west of the province. Seamus Heaney, in the opening page of *The Government of the Tongue,* shows the poet's sense of a similar concern in recounting how a recording session he was to have made for the BBC with the Ulster singer, David Hammond, was interrupted by a number of explosions in the city. The noise of sirens and ambulances made its own sad sound – a music against which the singer and his song seemed no longer appropriate. As a result, the recording session was abandoned. As Heaney puts it:

. . . the notion of beginning to sing at that moment when others were beginning to suffer seemed like an offence against their suffering.[9]

Art has always existed, of course, in a state of tension with the reality which it inhabits – indeed tension seems necessarily to be part and parcel of the best creative effort, as Yeats himself testified, whether of the opposites of personality, the inner conflicts which for Yeats were the quarrels which made for the highest creative endeavour: the mingling of contraries in 'our quarrel with ourselves'.[10] The struggle of poetry is, however, to some extent, an attempt to make marriages out of the divorces which result from these antithetical tensions, as it is the challenge to those of us who teach it to make that struggle mean something to pupils whose lives reflect divisions and divorces of a more literal and urgent sort.

The Government of the Tongue is an attempt on the part of an Ulster poet to explicate and to confront this challenge, both in the workshop of his own heart and from the understanding he has gained from his reading and experience of the literature of cultures other than those of Ireland. For the young Ulsterman, who began to write in the Northern Ireland of the Sixties at the start of the Troubles, questions surrounding the 'the present use' of poetry, particularly in societies torn by political and religious division, have an immediacy and compulsion far removed from the academic discussion others might make of it in the pages of a text book on literary theory. It is not surprising, indeed, that Heaney should return to this same theme in his most recent prose work – the collection of lectures he gave while he was Oxford Professor of Poetry – to consider the various forms of 'redress' which poetry provides to set against or counterbalance the pressures of reality.[11] What is the response which poets should give to the hecklers who demand that the poet's quest should attempt to reach out to the 'political destiny' of man rather than the deliberate creation of some unattainable destination in the holy city of the imagination? The poet, Brendan Kennelly, one of the best known public voices in modern Irish literature, in his review of Irish poetry since Yeats, confronts similar questions and asks:

How daring are Irish poets prepared to be? If we live in a murderous society should not our poetry reflect that fact? Does it? Or do poets create and cherish their own partitions?[12]

Should the answer to Kennelly's question be an insistence on the poet's right to survive 'amphibiously': simply to endure the hostile and oppressive 'times' he has to live in while simultaneously enjoying the Ivory Tower which he makes for himself in his art? Or are these questions less concerned with the poet's *right* to sing in the middle of suffering than they are with the *nature* of the song itself? In the personal embarrassment of Heaney and his singer friend, David Hammond, in the midst of the Belfast bombing, which resulted for both in an unwillingness if not also an inability to sing, is the implicit awareness among contemporary Irish poets of their professional and artistic predicament in our troubled times, as indeed for all poets in times of political crisis, suffering and horror of whatever kind. In examining this awareness in *The Government of the Tongue*, Heaney is reminded of Wilfred Owen – the English poet of the First World War – and the Russian dramatist Chekhov, a doctor, who experienced at first hand the suffering of young men in a penal camp – both writers whose experiences of war and suffering so bridge the gulf between art and life that, for them, the two are often indistinguishable: writers who so elevate the need to tell the truth above the lyric impulses of poetry to sing simply for its own sake, that Heaney, the young teacher, examining the well-known Owen poem, 'Dulce et Decorum Est', with a group of students, felt guilty and upset at applying anything resembling *literary* critical judgment to a poem whose *moral* integrity supersedes any other considerations of artistic 'decorum'. The challenge to poets to reconcile art with life has been, of course, particularly keenly felt in Eastern Europe, and Heaney quotes the words of the Polish poet, Zbigniew Herbert, writing in the aftermath of the ultimate horrors of the holocaust, in answer to it. Is not the only duty of the poet, Herbert suggests, to

. . . salvage out of the catastrophe of history at least two words, without which all poetry is an empty play of meanings and appearances, namely: justice and truth.[13]

Auden, MacNeice and other poets of the Thirties had asked the same question, following what for many of them had been the empty play – the ' superior amusement' with form and technique, language and meaning – of the Modernists, asserting that poets had more to do than indulge in esoteric experimentations and that their role was, in Auden's words, 'by telling the truth, to disenchant and disintoxicate'.[14] Are we then to conclude that it is the place of poetry solely to question? Is the answer to the question 'What do you want the poet for?', 'We want him to warn', and to use his artfulness, not to withdraw us from a world of suffering and division, but to make us more sensitive to it: to rub salt in the wounds we inflict on ourselves and others, rather than to heal? If this is the case, then we can question the meaning of the 'pleasure' of poetry that the Bullock Report – in company with many reports on the teaching of English – implies when it states:

We can sum up by saying that whatever else the pupil takes away from his experience of literature in school he should have learned to see it as a source of pleasure, as something that will continue to be a part of his life.[15]

Heaney returns later on in *The Government of the Tongue*, in further exploration of his own self-questioning, to quote from a poem
by Zbigniew Herbert, which, translated, is called 'The Knocker', a
poem in which the knocking of a stick is a constant reminder to the
poet of the integrity of his moral obligation:

> my imagination
> is a piece of board
> my sole instrument
> is a wooden stick
>
> I strike the board
> it answers me
> yes – yes
> no – no
>
> for others the green bell of a tree
> the blue bell of water
> I have a knocker
> from unprotected gardens
>
> I thump it on the board
> and it prompts me
> with the moralist's dry poem
> yes – yes
> no – no

The poem appears to deny the 'pleasure' principle – to the poet as
well as to his reader. As Heaney says, it

. . . ostensibly demands that poetry abandon its hedonism and fluency,
that it become a nun of language and barber its luxuriant locks down to
a stubble of moral and ethical goads.[16]

But this is not the whole story. In the act of writing the poem and
in its acknowledgement of the world of bells and gardens and trees,
it seems to assume another voice and to assert another kind of com-

mitment. In its 'yes – yes, no – no', the voice of the poem has the
ability both to deny and affirm the limited claims of both its lyric and
its moral compulsions and to do so simultaneously. It warns, of
course, but affirms in so doing that the poem itself is its own
universe, celebrating the independent and autonomous world of the
poem and the truer voice of art over the polemics of political and dry
moral statement. Heaney concludes of Herbert that he allows art
its 'rights', provided it also 'knows its limitations': ' "Go in peace",
his poem says. "Enjoy poetry as long as you don't use it to escape
reality" '.[17] 'Peace' is the word Heaney comes back to in his own
poetry, using the Coventry Patmore line, 'The end of art is peace', in
his poem, 'The Harvest Bow',[18] to point to the meaning or what he
calls the 'motto' of the plaited wheat straw in the golden corona, a
thing lovingly made by his father's hands, hands which know suffering and ageing but which, in the act of making and creating, resolve
the impermanences of life into the stillness and permanence of the
mellowed silence of art. The 'peace' offered by this frail device, handed
down to future generations to form part of their cultural heritage,
like the devices of poetry, is neither like experiencing a remote and
inert museum piece, however, nor the same as the peace of the cease-
fires which mark the end of wars in Europe or the cessations of
violence in Northern Ireland. In offering *resolutions* rather than *solu-
tions*, the ends of art have to be defined in their own terms . Its
'pleasure', like Heaney's 'peace', lies in the ways in which it can bring
to the chaos of life's experience another sort of order and another
kind of government. What then is this 'pleasure'? What kind of
'peace' can poetry offer to pupils who have known little in the way
of peace of the more literal kind emerging from the troubled days of
our recent history?

   In attempting to answer these questions, it is helpful to turn first
to the example of Ireland's greatest poet W. B. Yeats. The pleasure
which the poetry of one of the 'last romantics' as he referred to himself[19] offers to the readers of his poems or to the audiences of his plays
might easily be confused with the notion of an escape from the con-
strictions and limitations of life into some perfect and unattainable
'elsewhere'. The idealised love of 'He wishes for the Cloths of Heaven'[20]

is given in an image of woven cloths which are wrought of the ineffable and unreal 'night and light and the half-light', just as the wanderings of Aengus in his quest for the perfections of the 'Silver apples of the moon,/The golden apples of the sun'[21] are, as Yeats himself was to refer to them in his great poem 'Sailing to Byzantium',[22] journeys of the soul for 'unnatural' things which could never see the light of day. These are some of Yeats's 'masterful images', which, growing in 'pure mind',[23] come about because of the poet's quarrel with the real world, just as the poems in which they appear are representative of conflicts within the mind of the poet which were to preoccupy him for his entire life. The whole of Yeats's poetry is a territory vibrant with dramatic activity – a world of the imagination where perfect truth is enacted in images of birds 'Gyring, spiring to and fro'[24], a world where souls can clap their hands and sing, journey trembling on a cold road of guilt, or sail peacefully to the city of Byzantium – and it is not surprising that, in their urge towards a theatre, the poet felt a compulsion to attempt to translate them on to a real stage for others to share. It was in his search for *dramatis personae* and a form which could embody this vast drama of the imagination that Yeats was led to the cultural heritage of Ireland and to its mythological past – in particular, the stories of the great Ulster hero, Cuchulain, whose quests somehow appeared to parallel his own. The plays which result seem remote from life: *At The Hawk's Well*, *On Baile's Strand* and *The Only Jealousy of Emer*, for example, are plays of heroic affirmation of the right of individuals to assert the supremacy of their subjective selves – in maintaining their freedom, or in their search for an ideal and a transcendent and timeless world of truth – against an objective world of commercialism and superficiality which ultimately destroys them because it is blind to their values. The folly and blindness, both of the heroes in pursuit of their ideals and of the societies which destroy them, bind all of Yeats's plays into the tensions of a complex irony. But what is important in the context in which I have introduced them here, as it also is in learning how to respond to the plays, is the poet's desire to involve his audiences in finding the same needs in themselves.

Strange as they are – in the ritualised forms where the heaven's embroidered cloths of the poet's imagination are laid at the feet of his audiences in the stylised folding and unfolding of the cloths of the Japanese Noh play – Yeats's plays present a huge challenge to audiences brought up to expect problems of a different sort to be the real stuff of drama. The poet justified it, however, not because his objective was to bring to life some Golden Age that never was, or as he put it, the rituals of a lost faith, but because he believed that we, the audience, needed to be induced to find in ourselves something of the same myth-making process that motivated the ancient myth-makers, to reach states of mind where, as he put it in *Per Amica Silentia Lunae,* the heart might discover itself, by dramatising and experiencing all that man most lacks and all that he most dreads.[25] In other words, it is a part of the function of the plays to involve the audience in the creative act of playmaking, for it is in this that we will discover the artist in ourselves and the higher realities which connect us to and unify us with the 'collective unconscious' of the race. An equally important function for Yeats was that of helping to unite the divided society of the Ireland he inhabited, as torn apart by civil and political division as the Ireland of to-day. Consequently, Yeats refuses to identify art with real life by never allowing the audience to forget that they are experiencing an artefact. The Chorus figures which he uses to half-tell the plots of the plays as they unfold through the mouths of stylised and masked figures, remind us constantly that we are witnessing a story which has been told many times before and that, in the play, we are being invited to participate in its conclusion. The Fool and the Blind Man in *On Baile's Strand* – the play in which the hero kills his son and destroys himself as a result of being forced to take an oath of allegiance to the king – bind the thematic forces of the play into a dynamic structure and also give voice at times to the confused responses of the audience:

What a mix-up you make of everything, Blind Man! You were telling me one story, and now you are telling me another story. . . . How can I get the hang of it at the end if you mix everything at the beginning?[26]

Devices like this work at a superficial level in the theatre in helping to create suspense, but demonstrate at a more profound level of implication part of the creative process itself and embody all that the poet aimed for in attempting to establish a new form of verse drama in the Irish theatre at the beginning of the twentieth century, which, in common with the English theatre, suffered from what Yeats felt was a debasement of the imagination.

Poetry is for the poet a vital, if not also in the end, the ultimate way to attain truth. In its form, it does not discuss experience, analysing it and classifying it as philosophers, sociologists or political thinkers might do, but instead embodies it in symbolic form: like the Chinese ideogram, which, for Yeats's colleague and fellow poet, Ezra Pound, was a more exact form of language than European languages because it defined, for example, red, not in the form of an abstract definition such as 'Red is a colour', but by giving a series of images of red things such as iron rust, cherry, flamingo.[27] Similarly poetry, Pound felt, should give us truth exactly and directly in the images which contain it. Hence, when the poet Cuchulain says, at the end of the cycle of plays in which his quest is completed, ' I make the truth', he is asserting with Yeats what we should want the poet for in a world of shattered traditions, beliefs and institutions: a re-making and shaping of experience into the made-things of art. In inviting the Irish audiences of his plays to share this process in the myths of their common past, he is inviting them to discover something of the poet in themselves, for only in giving voice to universal aspirations and fears can people divided by creed and political persuasion be united in a common identity and find a peace which transcends the 'grey truth' of the actual world.

For Yeats, this process was worked out in the contexts of the world of Celtic legend which formed such an important part of the cultural heritage of Ireland. For Heaney, the ways in which, as he puts it, art can 'appease' or 'assuage' is a much more tangible and immediate process, evidenced in the craftsman's skill in the making of the harvest bow or in the Midas touch of the thatcher turning straw into the cottage roof. The son of a farmer, it is not surprising that it is to the metaphors of country things that Heaney turns in order to define the ways in which poetry earns its right to govern experience: just as farming is about digging, so poetry is about opening up unexpected and unedited communication between human nature and the reality we inhabit. It is a 'field work' of the imagination in which the poet hopes to raise

> A voice caught back off slug-horn and slow chanter
> That might continue, hold, dispel, appease:
> Vowels ploughed into other, opened ground,
> Each verse returning like the plough turned round.[28]

For Heaney, the ability of the poet to 'hold', 'dispel' and 'appease' is both his craft and his gift, a unique combination, both of what he has inherited from his past – something like Yeats's national consciousness in the form of his intuitive wisdom – and what he has acquired in the literate sense of his learning as a scholar of English literature and as a teacher. It is for him a complex blend of Irishness and Englishness, inextricably bound up with the land itself which similarly retains the marks of the history of the many invasions of the island in the rich language of its place names. It is to this past that Heaney turns to find the distinctive voice in which to make his own contribution to the particular kind of understanding which poetry can offer to those who have 'wintered out' the troubles of our recent and present history. For him, it is a search for the same sense of continuity as Yeats aimed for but, whereas the older poet found his in the ancient myths of Ireland, for Heaney it is in the formulation of what he called a personal 'mythos'.[29] This involved maintaining the efficacy of the watermarks of his own particular political and cultural colourings, in the process of finding a means of articulating and giving a sense of linguistic 'government' or order to the inchoate pieties and prejudices of his time. It is a getting to know both who he is and where he comes from, a verbal archaeology which digs deeply into the soil of personal and racial experience to unearth and so discover the wisdom which it retains in its buried treasures. It is thus in the search for a special kind of knowledge or understanding that Heaney comes to exercise what he called in an interview his 'conscience'. Explaining it he says:

One of the etymologies I like to make up about the word conscience is from 'con-scio', 'to will together', 'I will, You will, We will'. Conscience demands that we speak out what we all know together because we mustn't suppress it . . . by telling his own secrets the writer tells the secrets of the community. Their marginalised self, the secret self, somehow is pacified and they feel more at ease. I think if things are brought out into the open without aggression, as image rather than as accusation, then things are helped along. I think the writer has to invent a vicarious examination for other people.[30]

This, then, is Heaney's answer to the question of what we should want the poet for and the nature of the conscience which is at work in his own poetry. In his search for adequate verbal icons which can be brought out of the soil, his poetry is increasingly a journey outwards and backwards, a search northwards into the history of the invasions – not just of Ireland but of the whole of the British Isles – which resulted in the over-layering of different cultures and languages on to our indigenous landscape to make us who we are to-day. Inspired by discoveries made by a Danish anthropologist, P. V. Glob, he goes back in his poem, 'The Tollund Man',[31] to the early Iron Age in Northern Europe and makes a poetic journey to Aarhus in Denmark to contemplate the miraculously-preserved body of a man unearthed by turfcutters as they dug deeply into the soil – the 'last gruel of winter seeds' of his final meal still 'Caked in his stomach'. Glob had suggested that he was the victim of a ritual and violent killing – a human sacrifice made to appease a goddess in order to bring blessing to the soil, and it is this suggestion which provides for Heaney a powerful correlative for the suffering of his own time. From the ancient figure out of history, Heaney turns to modern Ulster and to the violent killings of equally anonymous young men from the present – ordinary labourers and farmers' sons, neither Cuchulains nor heroes, 'Stockinged corpses /Laid out in the farmyards' – and considers the parallels which link past and present in the continuity of human experience. And it is in the sense of the verbal pilgrimage which the poem becomes, that the poet offers a prayer: 'I could risk blasphemy', he says, 'and pray/Him to make germinate' the scattered flesh of those trailed for miles along the railway lines before meeting their end. 'To

make germinate' is the poet's plea for understanding: the only source
of reconciliation and regeneration which can transcend the senseless
slaughter of the helpless victims of violence. The Tollund man 're-
poses' in Aarhus, just as the poem achieves its appeasement in its
own sense of a 'sad freedom': a distanced perspective in which both
poet and reader can be momentarily released from the language of
accusation in which political dialogue is transacted, to attain greater
understanding of human experience in the images of art.

   T. S. Eliot, reviewing that great masterpiece of twentieth-century
fiction, *Ulysses,* described Joyce's use of the Homeric legend to overlay
the experiences of his Dubliners as a 'mythical method' and in so
doing made valuable comment on the usefulness of past cultures for
his own poetic method in *The Waste Land*:

In using myth, in manipulating a continuous parallel between contem-
poraneity and antiquity, Mr Joyce is pursuing a method which others
must pursue after him. . . . It is simply a way of controlling, of order-
ing, of giving a shape and a significance to the immense panorama of
futility and anarchy which is contemporary history.[32]

   Heaney's exercise of his poetic 'conscience' is an example of this
process in the mythical method of his own 'mythos': a blending and
joining of the 'I will' and the 'You will' into the 'We will together':
the personal voice of the poet and the national conscience becoming
the voice of a new European dimension of understanding:

> Out there in Jutland
> In the old man-killing parishes
> I will feel lost,
> Unhappy and at home.

   Brendan Kennelly is another poet who has pursued his own version of the Joycean mythical method so much admired by Eliot, in
his poetic exploration of the troubled history of Ireland through the
personal mythos he has made of the Cromwellian invasion[33] and the
story of Judas,[34] to confront and hence to provide greater understanding of the nature and the implications of Ireland's violence, both of

personal and national proportions. In the poems which result, he is, in his own words, 'breaking through the boundaries and categories' that separate the function of poetry from the oversimplifications of political, religious or other linguistic labelling, to restore to it a proper 'spirit of investigative uncertainty':[35]

To try to inhibit or limit that function is to do violence to the very nature of poetry, to make it the sweet, biddable, musical slave of our expectations. The poetry that deals with violence is more concerned with its *own* compulsions than with the expectations of others. It will not flatter or comfort or console; it will disturb, challenge, even threaten. Above all, it threatens our complacency.[36]

In poets such as Kennelly or Heaney, the integrity of vision which marks the compulsions of their poetry is asserted over the stereotypes which characterise so much of the visionless debate in which Irish politics, North and South, has trapped itself. 'Keep your eye clear as the bleb of the icicle' is the only 'epiphany' articulated in the 'swimming tongue' of the Viking longship, the image with which Heaney concludes his backward look into history in the title poem of his volume *North*,[37] and it is this – the compulsion of poetry to grasp at truth in exactitude of image, rather than by the certitudes of conviction in which the hard lines of division consolidate into the language-lock of immovable political agendas – which gives poets their right to govern in a troubled society. As Kennelly confidently asserts of poetry in its wider contexts of 'entering' and exploration:

> To be locked outside the image
> Is to lose the legends
> Resonant in the air
> When the bells have stopped ringing.
> If water soaks into the stone
> And sunlight is permitted to caress
> The worm and the root
> And the feather lodged in the bird's flesh
> Contributes to its flight

> It is right
> To enter the petal and the flame
> Live in the singing throat
> Mention a buried name
> And learn the justice of the skeleton.[38]

Returning to examine the place of poetry in Ulster's troubles in *The Redress of Poetry*, Heaney alludes to his poem from *Wintering Out*, 'The Other Side',[39] which examines the relationship between neighbouring farmers from both sides of the religious divide, and the embarrassment felt by the Protestant not wanting to disturb the family when he calls while they are engaged in the evening ritual of saying the rosary. Essentially it is a poem, not about religious difference, but about the boundaries of language which separate people: the barriers which Robert Frost ironically referred to as the 'good fences which make good neighbours'[40] in marking off the areas in relationships where discretion, mutual respect or simply the confusion of shyness, prohibit one from intruding verbally into territories of communication with the other, where words might fail or offend. Heaney's poem ends with the observing voice of the poet:

> Should I slip away, I wonder,
> or go up and touch his shoulder
> and talk about the weather
>
>
> or the price of grass-seed?

In the silence of the space which separates the last line from the rest is the suggestion of all the things which might be said to break down the 'good fences' and replace the safe exchanges of everyday farming conversation. Heaney says he was pleased with the poem, but stresses that it is not because of any 'useful' end it might be seen to serve:

. . . even if it showed Protestant and Catholic in harmony, it was not fundamentally intended as a contribution to better community relations. It had come out of creative freedom rather than social obligation, it was about a moment of achieved grace between people with different allegiances rather than a representation of a state of constant good-will in the country as a whole, and as such was not meant to be anything more than a momentary stay against confusion.[41]

The result of what Heaney calls 'creative freedom' rather than social or political obligation, the value of the poem is not then in any 'monstrous abuse of words' by which language might be manipulated into the fixed purposes of an ideological design or confused with the rhetoric in which so much of the hot air of political debate about the territory we inhabit takes place. Instead, in common with the modest aesthetic which underlies much great art, it offers what Heaney calls a moment of 'grace' in its 'stay against confusion', a phrase which he borrows from Robert Frost who first used it to describe 'the figure a poem makes'[42] in the momentary 'clarification' which his own poems attempted to set against the chaos of life.

Little wonder, then, that the same creative freedom and integrity of purpose, which united Yeats, Heaney and Kennelly in their separate myth-making endeavours, should have compelled others to turn to the landscape itself to find momentary clarification in images of reconciliation and regeneration. Among the many voices in which he writes, the classical scholar and one of Northern Ireland's best known poets, Michael Longley, has found a role for the poet in recording, with a painter's precision of eye, the landscape of County Mayo in the West of Ireland to which he regularly escapes from the troubles of his native Belfast. He writes poems of spare, clear image which delight in the truths that can be found in natural things – a harmonious world of mallards and kittiwakes, curlews and snipe, the flora and fauna of the west of the island – still remarkably free from the trappings of urban clutter:

> The spring tide has ferried jelly fish
> To the end of the lane, pinks, purples,
> Wet flowers beside the floating cow-pats.

The zig-zags I make take me among
White cresses and brookweed, lousewort,
Water plantain and grass of parnassus
With engraved capillaries, ivory sheen:
By a dry stone wall in the dune slack
The greenish sepals, the hidden blush
And a lip's red veins and yellow spots –
Marsh helleborine waiting for me
To come and go with the spring tide.[43]

Naming these things is for Longley, as it was for Patrick Kavanagh, from the other side of the border, 'the love act and its pledge',[44] committed as he was, no less than Longley, to recording the 'mystery' of his love for the ordinary things – the Dublin canals, the people and events of the indifferent County Monaghan countryside – without any undertow of sentimental or political claptrap. Rejecting the heroic myths of Yeats's poetic vocation, Kavanagh asserts his own comic vision to produce what Brendan Kennelly describes as 'a delightful body of poetry in which the mundane is transfigured by the mystical, and the mystical is earthed in the mundane.'[45]

But it seems that even the landscape of Northern Ireland cannot remain free from stereotyping. One of the foremost critics of Irish poetry, George Watson, a native Ulsterman now teaching in Aberdeen, writes with good-humoured resentment about the way in which the Ulster countryside and its towns, particularly the one in which he was brought up, Portadown – a stereotype of Ulster Protestantism – can be manipulated to become emblems of its sectarian divide.[46] He properly resents the identification of Protestant places with an absence of Irishness, a tendency which even a good poet like John Montague is guilty of in lines like these:

Through half of Ulster that Royal Road ran
Through Lisburn, Lurgan, Portadown,
Solid British towns, lacking local grace.[47]

In contrast, George Watson writes almost poetically and with considerable grace about his childhood as a young Catholic with an

English sounding name (George, not Eamonn or Sean, Watson, not O'Reilly or Kelly), living in Portadown – playing football, enjoying watching the trains go south to Dublin through places with Irish names like Newry, Goraghwood, Dundalk, Drogheda, and equally enjoying watching them go the other way to 'solid British' Belfast. Not unaware of the political problems of belonging to the religious minority in Portadown, however, it seems ironic to him that, when he went to a Catholic school in predominantly Catholic Armagh, he felt alienated among boys whose names were more Irish than his and who placed him in another minority, this time of less-than-Irish, for his love of soccer and cricket. Like Stephen Dedalus in James Joyce's *A Portrait of the Artist as a Young Man*, who was found 'guilty' and punished by his classmates for claiming that the immoral Byron was the best poet, Watson, too, feels isolated in his 'crime' of liking that most English of English writers, Thomas Hardy. He rightly concludes: ' There was no place in that Ireland for the flora and fauna of Portadown.' Now there is a real need in Northern Ireland for what is currently termed 'revisionism', both in reassessing our actual history and, as Edna Longley has courageously undertaken, our literary heritage as well:[48] a need to look at all of our past again in a perspective sceptical of the stereotypes in which, traditionally, our people, language and cultures have traditionally been cast, so that, as another well known critic, Roy Forster put it, the pieces might at least be rearranged in more 'surprising patterns'.[49] It is the capacity of the best poetry to do just that: to release us from imprisonment in the fifties of what George Steiner called, in another context,

. . . a linguistic contour which no longer matches, or matches only at certain ritual, arbitrary points, the changing landscape of fact.[50]

In offering his own challenge to such fixity in the aesthetic contexts of literature, George Watson quotes the comment made by Derek Mahon, a poet who, like him, deplores the fact that 'A lot of people who are important in Irish poetry cannot accept that the Protestant suburbs in Belfast are a part of Ireland' – any more, we might add, than they can accept that a Catholic with a Protestant name

might be a good nationalist and at the same time be happy in Union-
ist Portadown reading Thomas Hardy. Watson rightly commends
Mahon for his poetry of place – poetry which can, for example, like
'Courtyards in Delft', celebrate that most uncelebrated of Belfast Prot-
estant suburbs, Glengormley, by looking at it in the perspective of a
Dutch interior:

> I lived there as a boy and know the coal
> Glittering in its shed, late–afternoon
> Lambency informing the deal table,
> The ceiling cradled in a radiant spoon.[51]

'That is what love does to things', Kavanagh suggested, 'The
common and banal her heat can know'.[52] It is also what the keenly
observing eye of the poet, 'clear/as the bleb of the icicle', can do: by
releasing us from a world too closely pinned down by labels, the language of prejudice and political stereotyping, it enables us to see
ourselves and the places we inhabit in new and unexpected ways. To
assert the realities of our own place with the clarity of the poet's vision, insisting like Eavan Boland that the '*donnée*' of her poetic
landscape has to include the dustbins and the winter flowering jas-
mine of her neighbour's Dublin suburban garden[53], is to become
ourselves observers and participants in a new myth-making process
and the creators of our own 'mythos'. Impatient with the
simplifications of the rhetoric of traditional versions of history and
the grander themes of Irish heroic mythology which simply bandage
up the 'scalded memory'[54] of people and events into stereotyped
imitations of what really happened, Eavan Boland's poems are poems
of quest for a myth adequate to her uncompromising view of reality.
In terms reminiscent of Kavanagh she pleads of her muse:

> If she will not bless the ordinary,
> if she will not sanctify the common,
> then here I am and here I stay and then am I
> the most miserable of women.[55]

It is in assisting the process by which each of us can find a mythos adequate to our own experience of reality that we want and need poetry and poets, and a restoration of our cultural heritage to ourselves, devoid of the simplistic emblems of political weaponry.

At the beginning of this chapter, I posed the question of the place of poetry in the English curriculum – specifically in a troubled society – in terms of the teacher's role as well as the writer's. It is teachers' responsibilities and the responses of pupils in their own poems which are the particular focus of this book and to which I now want to turn. The examples I give here are representative of the book as a whole in that they are the result of work done by teachers and pupils from schools from both traditions in Northern Ireland and from the Republic of Ireland. Here, for example, a young boy of fourteen, from the perspective of the pupil, asks a similar question to that which troubled Seamus Heaney in the incident recounted at the beginning of *The Government of the Tongue*. In his poem, John is addressing, not a real poet, but one of Ireland's popular song writers, Phil Coulter, well known outside Ireland for Irish contributions to the Eurovision Song Contest, although better, perhaps, in Ireland, for his song about his native Londonderry, 'The Town I Loved so Well'. The poem sardonically dismisses such sentimental lyrics as grossly inappropriate to the world of suffering that John knows:

To Phil Coulter

You who write the song,
You are wrong.
Your romantic chords pluck a nostalgia
Which groans from a past,
Misrepresented and distorted.
Your indulgent 'Derry Air',
Languishing in the homely street scene
And the early morning mists,
Discredits our people.
The freshly dug graves of innocents
Refute your music,
Lilting over the screaming God-forsaken hills.
You dare make music
When orphans cry?

The boy has lost his father and uncle, both murdered by republican terrorists, so what authority, the poem asks, has the writer to sing in the midst of his heartache and what, we may add, can his education offer him? The answers to these questions are neither instant nor easy, though the authors of the Common Curriculum for Northern Ireland have made a bold attempt to address them.

The Northern Ireland curriculum has much in common with its counterparts for England and Wales, but is, however, also distinctively different in that it attempts to address the problems of a divided community through its Cross-Curricular Themes, such as Education for Mutual Understanding, Cultural Heritage and greater European awareness. Couched though they are in educational rather than literary language, they have much in common with directions taken by both Yeats and Heaney in asserting their confidence in the place of poetry as a vital way of understanding reality. The Cultural Heritage theme, for example, has at its basis much of what Yeats hoped for in appealing, in his plays and the myths of which they were made, to the shared memory of the race as a vital way by which people, divided by creed and political aspiration, might discover something of their common identity, just as the consciousness of a wider European context of culture, language and history enabled Heaney to find symbols adequate to a clearer understanding of who and what we are in the pluralities of our European past. This view of the values inherent in a shared cultural past and the necessity for bringing it into a vital relationship with the present has, however, to be distinguished from the Cultural Heritage 'model' of English teaching and the place of literature within it as it was described and rejected by educationalists like John Dixon in the Sixties. In the now famous Dartmouth Seminar on the teaching of English which took place in 1966, Dixon rejected what he perceived to be a commonly held view of English as essentially about transmitting and fostering knowledge of the cultural heritage of the past as it was enshrined in the best of the 'Great Tradition' of English literature, whether it is that defined by F. R. Leavis or government working groups set up to determine which authors our pupils should read. In its place, Dixon favoured a 'personal growth' approach to the subject: a concept of language development in which the child is seen to be the centre of the learning process, the chief aim of which should be to encourage and promote a personal and individualised view of the world.[56]

The rationale for the 'personal growth' model and its association with what is now often described as the 'trendy' or 'progressive' Sixties are too complex to describe here, as are the reasons why Dixon himself later came to recognise its limitations in the revision of his earlier strenuous defence of it.[57] What is important to emphasise, however, is that in overcoming the weaknesses of the 'personal growth' approach, it was not simply a matter of reinstating the 'traditional' view of cultural heritage, but of having a better understanding of how personal growth comes about. The Bullock committee, for example, in reviewing different approaches to English teaching in *A Language for Life* and, in particular, the period of the Sixties in which Dixon was such a central figure, saw dangers in overemphasising a child-centred view of English in which language learning takes place 'naturally', by discovery, without intervention by the teacher, in some 'free' or 'creative' environment. While it is obvious that the child has to be at the centre of the learning process, it should also be equally true that personal growth cannot be an entirely subjective process. Since learning takes place within a particular culture, (whatever its limitations and need for change), we have to acknowledge that the individual pupil is not free to grow independently of the society in which he lives. We are all what we are because of the experience which we share with others in our present and as a result of what we have inherited from our past. George Steiner understood this well, placing his own emphasis on the importance of the past in arriving at a coherent sense of who we are in the present:

Each new historical era mirrors itself in the picture and active mythology of its past or of a past borrowed from other cultures. It tests its sense of identity, of regress or new achievement, against that past. The echoes by which a society seeks to determine the reach, the logic and the authority of its own voice, come from the rear. Evidently, the mechanisms at work are complex and rooted in diffuse but vital needs of continuity. A society requires antecedents.[58]

In such a view, 'cultural heritage' is not an inert body of knowledge which the cultivated few have the obligation to hand on 'intact' to succeeding generations, but is itself actively involved in the formulating processes of defining identity, the value systems and the social objectives of the new. Personal growth, like the growth of society, involves bringing the past into vital relationship with the present, not discarding it. Interestingly, however, the same point was being made at the Dartmouth Seminar in the Sixties:

Clearly we must recognise the importance of the instinct of origination, but an education based on the training of the instinct is not enough. Language conveys to a child an already prepared system of values and ideas that form his culture. Each new generation is not a new people; we are what we are because we are able to share a past, in a common heritage, not simply because of our ability to communicate in the present and share the excitement of innovation.[59]

The real 'growth' of the individual is, as both comments indicate, an adjustment between the private and the public; what sociologists call 'acculturation' is the merging of the individual perception of the 'me' and 'mine' with what is 'ours' and what is shared. In this, the past is as important as the present in the shaping of an independent and personal view of the world.

Since it is, of course, through language that such formulations take place, it is ultimately a pupil's language resources which will determine the quality of the adjustment or growth which takes place. Just as the literature of the past should not be seen solely as museum pieces to be treasured as relics of our inheritance, however precious, so, too, language has to be bound up with the formulating process through which the experiences which we inherit from our past – in both Yeats's definition of cultural heritage as well as Heaney's interpretations of what Eliot referred to as 'the mind of Europe'[60] – are brought into active relationship with the present. This is why, in addition to the reading of poetry, pupils should learn to write it, as the next chapter of this book will seek to demonstrate. It is on this territory that poets, past and present, meet and join with the authors of our common curriculum in a confident assertion of the place of literature in helping John, the young poet referred to earlier, and his contemporaries, to come to terms with the confusing world they live in – and not just the politically divided society of Northern Ireland. In his essay, 'Irish Poetry since Yeats', Brendan Kennelly, himself a teacher with a humanity and integrity of purpose of a special kind, commends the fact that so many of our young pupils in schools in the North are writing their own poetry about violence, energetically asserting the need for all poets to confront such experiences with honesty and courage. He goes on to make the vital connection between poetry and education in the mutual understanding which can result from such acts of open exploration:

Poetry is the deepest kind of education there is, a conscious, structured, logical, inspiring illumination of the various darknesses in us all. Poetry which is fully alive is always on a threshold, making fresh assaults on ignorance, intolerance and evil so that concepts and practices of tolerance may be endlessly refreshed and re-invigorated, even as intense, rhythmical language is enjoyed and reflected on.[61]

Yeats failed, as we know, in his attempt to translate his private convictions into the 'usefulness' of a public stage, and he went on in scorn of what he perceived to be the 'Paudeens' who rejected his efforts, to cultivate what he ironically termed the 'wasteful virtues'[62] of his art for a more sympathetic and better-informed minority. But his failure does not detract from the value of his efforts, however, nor from those of the authors of our new curriculum, though, of course, only history will judge how successfully all of us concerned to make it work may be in educating a new generation of Irish men and women.

What is important for John, however, is the confidence and faith he has found from his appreciation of poetry and how its language operates as well as that of the popular culture to which he is also exposed, in the power and integrity of poetry as art to govern experience, in feeling objectified as image, – asserted by Yeats and later by Heaney to what he calls the point of 'arrogance'[63] – rather than manipulated as accusation, by bomb, bullet or political bombast. What the young poet, in his poem, 'To Phil Coulter', exposes is his awareness of the shams of feeling exploited in the sentimental song. More importantly, perhaps, in the *objectification* of the experience which he undergoes in the writing of it, he is able momentarily to cope with his own feeling by submerging and generalising it into the shared experience of others, similarly orphaned. In such objectification, his poem gains something of Heaney's kind of 'peace' or Frost's momentary 'stay against confusion' through the submerging of himself and his experiences in what T. S. Eliot referred to as the 'impersonality' of the mature artist. For Eliot – and hence also for John – this is not a 'turning loose of emotion' but 'an escape from emotion'[64] into a world where, as Wallace Stevens put it, 'the world's poverty and change and evil' undergo a 'purging' in the 'present perfecting' of the poem.[65] What is important, too, is that pupils learn that such generalising tendencies as these are not the same as the generalisations made in statements of ideology from the safety and superiority of the territories of our own shut minds or in the rhetorical devices of language in which Yeats claimed that our quarrels with others are conducted. Poetry should not be 'a diagram of political attitudes', Heaney stated, asserting instead, to a point of 'triumphalism',[66] his faith in the language of poetry as art to explore the ironies which challenge the dreadful certainties of fact and the predatory agendas of those with a political axe to grind. Sharing something of Kennelly's spirit of investigative uncertainty, Heaney aptly sums it up :

There's nothing extraordinary about the challenge to be in two minds.[67]

Such irony is revealed in the following poem, this time by a young Protestant girl, a poem which at once affirms the cultural traditions enshrined in the Protestant Twelfth-of-July commemorations, while simultaneously expressing her own sense of their absurdity in the oversimplification of the events of history on which they are based:

THE TWELFTH-DAY PARADE

The procession curls its way
Through the long line of spectators,
The pageant boldly announcing

This day belongs to us.
Coloured banners tug the morning air,
And the thump of drums,
The rhythm of Protestantism,
Resound through the streets.
Collaretted, the marching brethren
Step out in symmetrical remembrance
Of a river, a battle, and a king.

'A river, a battle, and a king' is for many the sum of what is known about that period of Ulster's history: simple facts welded, not only into symmetrical remembrance in the annual processions, but too often as well into the strict conformity of the hard lines of 'no surrender' political affirmation. The poem describes the parade with what Joyce might have called 'scrupulous meanness':[68] the scrupulous observer who is both at one with the festive spirit of the participants in its rituals and at the same time 'impersonal' in the clear-eyed judgment which the poem makes of it.

The knocking of Zbigniew Herbert's stick was a reminder to the Polish poet of the seriousness of his obligation to tell the truth, a demand which his poem simultaneously accepted and refused, rejecting the 'moralist's dry poem' by affirming the place of blue bells, water and gardens in the poet's broader vision. And it is with the lyric impulse in Ireland's youngest writers that I would like to conclude this chapter. Here is an eight-year old poet, celebrating in her poem the famous Mourne Mountains which, in the well-known song, sweep down to the sea, but more importantly for her, stop at her school playground on their way. She is speculating about their shape and the names of the smaller peaks which adjoin the tallest, Slieve Donard. She manipulates her knowledge and understanding of the cultural heritage of Ireland in the legend of the famous giant, Finn McCool, in the language of her own myth-making, to write a poem which might well have delighted Yeats himself:

The View from our School

Standing in the playground
I can see Slieve Donard, the mountain,
With Thomas his son.
Just near, the valley Blackstairs is flowing.
Every time I see the Saddle
I wonder if it gets its name from Finn McCool.
Did he ride the mountains like a horse
And flatten out the valley in between?
Up from the Saddle is Mummy Commedagh,
Swooping down to meet Slieve Donard.
There they stand, hand in hand,
Looking down over the school.

In the same way, her classmate looks at the gulls in the school yard
with the keen naturalist's eye, knowing that they look different in the
winter, and delights that she has found a correlative for the spots on
the sides of their heads in the little radio which she listens to on her
headphones:

Our School Yard

Black headed gulls come every day
To our school yard.
They're our dustmen,
For they pick up all our rubbish.
Their uniform is not green like ours,
It's white with a dark brown cap.
But in winter they leave off their caps –
    Silly birds!
And wear their Walkmans instead.

One of Yeats's finest poems, 'Sailing to Byzantium', deplores the
tatters that old age makes of the body and the fact that only the
young are free to celebrate the pleasures of life and time in 'Whatever

is begotten, born and dies'. For the poet, the only recourse is to reject all natural life and seek instead transcendence in the permanent and perfect state of an afterlife of art. So in the poem Yeats sails to Byzantium, choosing for his habitation to become a part of an elaborate mosaic, in the form of a golden bird on a golden branch, perpetually singing. What is interesting, however, is that, having achieved fulfilment of his quest, the source and the object of his singing will be the celebration of the life of time from which he has departed: '. . . what is past, or passing, or to come'. Arrival at Byzantium is thus a fusion of affirmation and denial, perfection of the life and the art, resolvable, however, only in the world of the poem itself. And it is its unique ability to mediate between worlds – the mundane and the mystical, the real and the ideal, the private and the social, hope and despair, and all life's contradictions and conflicts – in the made-image of the poem, which is the ultimate goal of all good poetry. Yeats justifies his quest in lines at the beginning of the poem which sum up all that I have been trying to say here:

> An aged man is but a paltry thing,
> A tattered coat upon a stick, unless
> Soul clap its hands and sing, and louder sing
> For every tatter in its mortal dress.

'Words alone are certain good', declared the poet in his much earlier poem, 'The Song of the Happy Shepherd',[69] celebrating with the happy shepherd the capacity of poetry to clap and sing over the tatters of experience, not by providing answers to it in the form of the 'grey truths' of practical or political wisdom, but by means of the 'melodious guile' of song, its own particular kind of 'redress', to use Heaney's term for it. In explaining his choice of the word, Heaney explores the many dictionary meanings of 'redress', both as noun and verb, and shows how, as noun, its meaning suggests a 'reparation' for wrong or a compensation. As verb, however, the dictionary states, 'to set upright again, to raise or to erect', and figuratively, ' to restore, to re-establish.' Among all these meanings, it is in the latter affirmative function of image as 'redress' in doing and being that

Heaney defines the distinctive nature of poetic order, not as moral reparation, but in the governing of it in the jurisdiction of a form which both liberates and orders in the surprise of its newness:

. . . I want to celebrate its given, unforeseeable thereness, the way it enters our field of vision and animates our physical and intelligent being in much the same way as those bird-shapes stencilled on the transparent surfaces of glass walls or windows must suddenly enter the vision and change the direction of the real birds' flight. In a flash the shapes register and transmit their unmistakable presence, so the birds veer off instinctively. An image of the living creatures has induced a totally salubrious swerve in the creatures themselves. And this natural, heady diversion is also something induced by poetry and reminds me of a further (obsolete) meaning of 'redress' . . . 'to bring back . . . to the proper course.' In this 'redress' there is no hint of ethical obligation; it is more a matter of finding a course for the breakaway of innate capacity, a course where something unhindered, yet directed, can sweep ahead into its full potential.[70]

It is the potential of poetry and poems to fulfil these functions – as things made as well as in things said – that this book celebrates: a world of the melodious guile of an artefact where the common and banal things of experience can be so manipulated that they etch themselves into our consciousness to provide us with new meanings, new perspectives on the literal world of truth. In asserting this obligation – to sing above the noise of the workaday world – poetry offers to all who teach it and write it both a 'major channel of experience' and true pleasure. And it is in its 'thereness', its power to animate our physical and intelligent beings, that we are provided with the only answer which is worth giving to the question of what we want the poet for and why we should encourage our pupils to write their own poetry .

[1]   T. E. Hulme, *Speculations: Essays on Humanism and the Philosophy of Art,* edited by Herbert Read (London: K. Paul, Trench, Trubner, 1924), p.147.

[2]   *Proposals for the English Curriculum.* Report of the English Working Group (Belfast: NICC, 1989), Chapter 2,3.12, p.14.

3 *Half our Future* [the Newsom Report]. Report of the Central
   Advisory Council for Education (England) (London: HMSO,
   1963), Paragraph 462, p.152.

4 *A Language for Life* [the Bullock Report]. Report of the
   Committee of Inquiry appointed by the Secretary of State for
   Education and Science (London: HMSO, 1975), 1.4, p.4.

5 T. S. Eliot, *The Sacred Wood: Essays on Poetry and Criticism*
   (London: Methuen, 1920), p.ix.

6 *ibid.*

7 These ideas are contained in *Scrutiny,* the journal which
   Leavis edited, as well as in *Revaluation* (London: Chatto and
   Windus, 1936), and *The Great Tradition* (New York: New
   York University Press, 1948).

8 *A Language for Life,* 1.9, p.7.

9 Seamus Heaney, *The Government of the Tongue* (London:
   Faber, 1988), p. xi..

10 W. B. Yeats, *Per Amica Silentia Lunae* (London: Macmillan,
   1918), p.21.

11 Seamus Heaney, *The Redress of Poetry: Oxford Lectures*
   (London: Faber, 1995).

12 Brendan Kennelly, *Journey into Joy: Selected Prose,* edited by
   Ake Persson (Newcastle upon Tyne: Bloodaxe, 1994), p.44.

13 *The Government of the Tongue,* p.xviii.

14 W. H. Auden, 'Writing', *The Dyer's Hand* (London: Faber,
   1963), p.27.

15 *A Language for Life,* Chapter 9. 28, p.137.

16 *The Government of the Tongue,* pp.99,100.

17 *ibid.,* pp. xviii, xix.

18 Seamus Heaney, *Field Work* (London: Faber, 1979), p.58.

19 'Coole Park and Ballylee', *Collected Poems* (London:
   Macmillan, 1967), pp.275, 276

20 *ibid.,* p.81

21 *ibid.,* p.66

22 *ibid.,* pp.217, 218.

23 'The Circus Animals' Desertion', *ibid.,* p.392.

24 'The Two Trees', *ibid.,* pp.54,55.

25 *Per Amica Silentia Lunae,* p.22.

26 W. B. Yeats, *Collected Plays* (London: Macmillan, 1977), p.252.

27 Gertrude Patterson, *T. S. Eliot: Poems in the Making*
   (Manchester: Manchester University Press, 1971), pp.63 ff.

28 Seamus Heaney, Glanmore Sonnets 11, *Field Work*, p.34.

29 'Unhappy and at Home', interview with Seamus Deane, *The Crane Bag*, No. 1 (1977), 61-67. Reprinted in *The Crane Bag Book of Irish Studies*, 1977-1981 (Dublin: Blackwater Press, 1982), 66-72.

30 Interview in *The Irish News*, 2 July, 1987.

31 Seamus Heaney, *Wintering Out* (London: Faber,1972), pp.47,48.

32 T. S. Eliot,'Ulysses, Order and Myth', *The Dial*, lxxv (1923), 480-83.

33 Brendan Kennelly, *Cromwell: a Poem* (Dublin: Beaver Row, 1983).

34 Brendan Kennelly, *The Book of Judas: a Poem* (Newcastle upon Tyne: Bloodaxe, 1991).

35 Preface to *The Book of Judas*, p.9.

36 Brendan Kennelly, 'Poetry and Violence' in *Journey into Joy*: p.44

37 'North', *North* (London: Faber, 1975), pp.19,20.

38 'Entering', *A Time for Voices: Selected Poems 1960-1990* (Newcastle upon Tyne: Bloodaxe, 1990), p.30.

39 *Wintering Out*, pp.34-36.

40 Robert Frost, *Selected Poems*, edited by Ian Hamilton (Harmondsworth: Penguin, 1973), p.43.

41 *The Redress of Poetry*, p.194.

42 Robert Frost, 'The Figure a Poem Makes', quoted by Laurence Thompson, 'Robert Frost's Theory of Poetry', in *Robert Frost: A Collection of Critical Essays*, edited by James Cox, (New York: Prentice Hall Inc, 1962), pp.20-21.

43 Michael Longley, *Poems 1963-1983* (London: Faber,1985), p.157.

44 Patrick Kavanagh, *Collected Poems* (London: Martin Brian and O'Keeffe, 1972), p.153.

45 Brendan Kennelly, 'Irish Poetry since Yeats', *Journey into Joy*, p.56.

46 George Watson, 'Landscape in Ulster Poetry' in *The Poet's Voice*, edited by Gerald Dawe and John Wilson Forster (Belfast: Institute of Irish studies, 1991), pp.1-15.

47 quoted by George Watson, ibid., p.8.

48 Edna Longley, *The Living Stream* (Newcastle upon Tyne: Bloodaxe, 1994).

49 Lecture by Roy Forster, quoted by George Watson, 'Landscape in Ulster Poetry', p.10.

50 George Steiner, *After Babel* (Oxford: Oxford University Press, 1975), pp.18,19.

51 quoted by George Watson, 'Landscape in Ulster Poetry', p.12.

52 *Collected Poems,* p.153.

53 Eavan Boland, 'Envoi', *Selected Poems* (Manchester, Carcanet, 1989), pp.89,90.

54 'Mise Eire', *ibid.,* p.71.

55 *ibid.,* p. 90.

56 John Dixon, *Growth through English,* 2nd edition (London: Oxford University Press for the National Association for the Teaching of English, 1967)

57 *Growth Through English: Set in the Perspective of the Seventies,* Oxford Studies in Education, 3rd edition (Oxford: Oxford University Press, 1975).

58 George Steiner, *In Bluebeard's Castle: Some Notes Towards the Re-Definition of Culture* (London: Faber, 1971), p.1.

59 Glyn Lewis, 'The Teaching of English', Working Party IV, *Dartmouth Seminar Papers,* N.A.T.E. 1969, also quoted in David Allen, *English Teaching since 1965: How Much Growth?* (London: Heinemann Educational, 1980), p.40.

60 T. S. Eliot, 'Tradition and the Individual Talent', *The Egoist,* VI (September-October,1919), reprinted in *Selected Essays* (London: Faber, 1951), p.16.

61 Brendan Kennelly, *Journey into Joy,* p.64.

62 *Collected Poems,* p.113.

63 *Preoccupations: Selected Prose 1968 - 1978* (London: Faber, 1980), p.217.

64 'Tradition and the Individual Talent', *Selected Essays* (London: Faber, 1951), pp.13-22.

65 Wallace Stevens, 'Andagia', from *Opus Posthumous,* reprinted in *Modern Poets on Modern Poetry,* edited by James Scully (London: Collins, 1966), p.156.

66 *Preoccupations,* pp. 217, 219.

67 *The Redress of Poetry,* p.202.

68 James Joyce, *Letters,* II, edited by Richard Ellman (London: Faber, 1966), p.134.

69 *Collected Poems,* pp.7, 8.

70 *The Redress of Poetry,* p.15.

CHAPTER TWO

'That poetry is made with words'

Poets, Poetry
and
the Craft of Writing

THE EMPHASIS OF THE LAST CHAPTER was placed on the light which poets themselves could throw on the particular nature of the 'order' or 'government' which poetry confers on the chaotic nature of experience – personal, social, or national – and on the links which could be made between their thinking and the more tentative, though no less valid, responses of some of the young writers whose work is included in this collection. It is time now to turn to the application of such knowledge and understanding to classroom practice in attempting to show how such responses may come about.

To start with, we must return to the comment from the Report of the Northern Ireland Working Party for English, which placed poetry 'at the heart of work in English because of the quality of language at work on experience which it offers'.[1] It is as a direct consequence of this, that from Key Stage 1 onwards, emphasis is placed on the need to include a wide range of poetry within the literature programme of the English Curriculum and to demand that pupils at all levels should be required to write their own verse. The Report makes the vital connection which exists between the values of literature, the various modes of language which it brings together and the effect of both, not only in broadening pupils' emotional, environmental and cultural experience, but on the range of their expressive language skills as well. The Report of the Committee of Inquiry into the Teaching of Language under the chairmanship of Sir John Kingman, whose recommendations formed the embryology of the substance of the

English Curriculum for England and Wales, and hence also for Northern Ireland, earlier made the same connection and the Northern Ireland Working Party acknowledges its source:

. . . as children read more, write more, discuss what they have read and move through the range of writing in English, they amass a store of images from half-remembered poems, of lines from plays, of phrases, rhythms and ideas. *Such a reception of language allows the individual greater possibilities of production of language.*[2] (italics mine)

The last sentence is of the greatest importance – as will be evidenced in the examples of writing given later in this chapter. At first sight, however, the Kingman comment, together with the new context in which it is reiterated in the Northern Ireland Report, might appear no more than an updated endorsement of the approach to poetry and the writing of it popularly referred to as 'creative writing', favoured by teachers in the Sixties. But as the introduction to this book makes clear, there are significant differences. The Northern Ireland Proposals, again echoing Kingman's comment, later taken up by Professor Cox in his Reports for England and Wales, see the English classroom as a 'workshop' in which the role of the teacher is not solely that of providing a stimulus for writing, nor the sole audience and assessor of the product, but an active participant in the process, a 'master craftsman' working alongside pupils as 'apprentices',[3] going through each stage of the writing with them, demonstrating the importance of learning the craft in which they are collaboratively engaged. The idea of the classroom as a workshop is not new, of course, but the image of the craftsman working with young apprentices places a distinctively different emphasis on the creative process from the various forms of spontaneous and immediate utterance adopted by those who favoured a more 'free' approach, connecting it more with a craft or a trade which can be improved by effort as well as from the example and experience of the skilled practitioners from whom it is learned. The Northern Ireland Report makes reference to the views of Sandy Brownjohn, wife of the poet Alan Brownjohn, on the subject, in a comment which reinforces these ideas:

I see the teaching of poetry writing to children as the teaching of skills and techniques almost as much as the use of original ideas – a love of language and the excitement of exploring its possibilities, making it work for you.[4]

Such a concept of writing and the teacher's part in it is clearly distinguishable from the 'creative writing' process of the Sixties, as it was often misunderstood and practised, where the value of children's writing lay more in the fact that they did it at all than in any conscious workmanship in what they were doing. The new approach is consistent with the concepts on which the whole of the English curriculum for schools within the National Curriculum for England and Wales and the Common Curriculum for Northern Ireland are based, but before going on to look more closely at the nature of these skills, it is useful here to examine in greater detail something of the wider learning context in which the craft of writing takes place.

Central to all of the components of the new English curriculum is the twofold demand that teachers themselves need to be more knowledgeable about the language processes in which their pupils are engaged – one of the main emphases of the earlier Bullock Report – and that some sense of progression has to be planned for in English, in order to avoid what Geoffrey Summerfield described as the 'teaching from hand to mouth, a chronic non-co-ordination of learning and a policy of *ad-hoc* excitements' which, in his view, characterised so much of the English teaching of his day.[5] Summerfield properly called for more explicit structuring of language development in the classroom in his demand for 'articulated progression' in English, a demand for a greater knowledge of the incremental processes involved in the acquisition of increased linguistic competence in all aspects of the curriculum so that, as the Northern Ireland Proposals were later to put it, pupils' progress in English would not be 'left to chance'.[6]

The question as to whether *stages* in language development can be identified and how such a process takes place is a complex issue. Implicit in the Programmes of Study for the new curriculum – which attempts to define different levels of attainment which can be appropriately expected of pupils at each key stage of schooling – is the recognition that some sense of sequence can and should be planned for, while, at the same time, rightly asserting that English is *recursive:*

. . . that development is often charted not by the acquisition of new skills but by a more sophisticated ability to handle familiar ones.[7]

A great deal of research has been done in the area of how to achieve progress in language development, paradoxically indeed, much of it taking place in the 'progressive' or 'trendy' Sixties of which Summerfield at the time, as indeed others since, have been so critical. Vygotsky, for example, in his linguistic research, made an important contribution to the thinking of those who, like Bullock and later Kingman, stressed the need for greater awareness on the part of teachers of the processes involved in ensuring pupils' increased handling of language as new demands were made on their language resources from one learning context to another. There are problems in defining specific linguistic goals to match the chronological stages of a child's development, however, as the initial outrage which followed the first attempt by the DES Inspectorate Report in *English from 5 to 16* was to indicate.[8] On the one hand, apart from the obvious danger of getting the sequence wrong, there are the greater problems of itemising specific skills in sequences which threaten the interrelatedness of language types in a curriculum which, as the Northern Ireland group also correctly states, is *holistic* as well as recursive. On the other hand, not to attempt it at all can lead to the very 'non-co-ordination of learning' to which Geoffrey Summerfield referred in his demand for a greater sense of 'articulated' or explicit progression in English.

The Nuffield Foundation Project of 1964 (which became the Schools' Council Programmes in Linguistics and English Teaching) set out to investigate how far new linguistic approaches to language – in this case, the work of M. A. K. Halliday, Professor of Linguistics at University College, London – could be of help to teachers in planning their new curriculum.[9] Most interesting, however, in the context in which I introduce it here, was the work of J. C. Moffett, whose *Teaching the Universe of Discourse* in 1968[10] must have been one of the earliest attempts to describe and itemise the line of progression which Bullock was later to identify as a language process running from narrative to generalising, from concrete to abstract. Moffett identifies two 'ladders' of ascent in his language chain. The first describes a sequence in the relation of the 'speaker' to his 'audience', the second, the speaker's relationship to his 'subject'. In the first, he places 'reflection' on the first rung: the stage at which the speaker (or writer) is thinking or reflecting to himself. The second is 'conversation', the stage at which he is communicating directly to a friend or friends. The third stage is 'correspondence': communication between speaker and others, known to the speaker but not present; and finally, 'publication': where the speaker is communicating with an unknown audience. In the second ladder of ascent, describing the relationship of the language user to his material, four stages are again identified: recording (what is happening or what is observed); reporting or narrating (what has happened); generalising (what happens); and logical argumentation, theorising, or speculating (what might or should happen). The interest of such a model as this is not, of course, in the rigid application of it to classroom practice. Indeed, where Moffett appears to have gone wrong was in his suggestion that progression in his ladders of ascent is entirely a linear process and that skill in one kind of language could not take place until the one before it had been thoroughly mastered. 'Publication', for example, should not be expected of pupils before the secondary stages of schooling – a claim which the writing produced here will show to be invalid.

What proves significant in linguistic research of this kind, however – particularly in the light of the Programmes of Study for English and in the levels of attainment which they indicate as appropriate for each age group – are the *directions* which Moffett indicates in his ladders, directions which are helpful to teachers, not just in planning a curriculum for the different key stages of pupils' maturation, either in the longer or the shorter term, but in determining the sequential direction of teaching and in helping to account for the success or otherwise of a lesson or series of lessons. With regard to writing, this is important, whether the purpose of the writing task is functional, as the following example will show, or poetic, as it is the aim of this chapter to demonstrate.   A class of ten year olds had been asked to write the instructions for playing football. Andrew produced the following:

My favourite Game is football. It is well none all over the world. It is not just a kids Game it is a Gown up game to, there are lots and lots of teams in Britain. There is Liverpool and Exeter City and York City and West Ham United and Many more team these team meat up and play against each over it. Ends like 3 v 1 and things like that. This is how you play. You have a field and up each end of the pitch you have a goal. And the field has lines. Thing you got to do is score in the goals. I mean you have to kick a ball in the Net and Goal keeper got to you from doing this. You elevan Players in each side if you are playing Proffesinill. And Ill Tell you the Rules. If the ball goes off the pitch it is a throwing. And if you kick some man you have a three kick . . . . Ill tell you the Bisians theres a Goal keeper and Defenders, midfielders, Strikers,Wingers, right Back, Left back, and theres more too and that how you play football, and if you pracktise you may play for a profeinel, one day.[11]

The problem with this writing is not just its lack of secretarial skills, though Andrew clearly has difficulty with spelling and punctuation. In tackling his problems, however, the question the teacher must address is whether or not he is being asked to write at a level of exposition for which he has had inadequate preparation. Andrew clearly knows a great deal about football but is finding it hard to extricate himself from the expressive and personal account he is giving. Is he ready to learn how to manipulate the passive voice as a way of avoiding the first-person 'Now I'll tell you'? Does he know what instructions or rules look like? Has he had enough models to learn from? Would a diagram help his explanation? Could he learn about connectives which would enable him to avoid beginning so many sentences with 'And'? Does he know the 'you' for whom he is writing? He is clearly engaged here at the level of 'correspondence' rather than 'publication'. His spelling suggests that he has derived his knowledge of the game from oral rather than written sources. If this is the case, does he then read enough? These are all important questions, and answers can only be found to them if the teacher has enough knowledge about how language must operate in this particular context and the processes by which Andrew and the rest of his class might be brought to acquire it. Such knowledge and understanding of how language operates in poetry is equally necessary if teachers are to respond to pupils' poetry in ways which will enable them to make progress in the writing of it.

The concept of the language process as it was described by Moffett in the too-rigid sequence of his ladders and, more flexibly, in the principles which underlie Programmes of Study for the new curriculum, both run parallel to the formulating view of language as it is described by Bullock:

To bring knowledge into being is a formulating process, and language is its ordinary means, whether in speaking or writing or the inner monologue of thought. Once it is understood that talking and writing are means of learning, those more obvious truths that we learn also from other people listening and reading will take on a fuller meaning and fall into a proper perspective.[12]

It was in the context of learning within the whole school curriculum that Bullock demanded greater understanding on the part of the teacher of the processes involved in the development of pupils' formulating language skills in writing, but the message is the same whether the purpose of the written act is functional or transactional, as the above example illustrates, or creative. For Bullock, 'knowledge' is not something which exists independently in the mind of the knower, and for which written language is necessary only to transfer it from one state to another for the purposes of communication; instead, knowledge is itself formulated, or, as Bullock put it, 'brought into being' by the learner through the efforts of his own linguistic processes: from personal reflection to other forms of collaborative communication – conversation and discussion – and from notetaking and drafting to the more formal written structures by which such knowledge is transacted. Bullock was right in his demand, not just in the new emphasis which he placed on the nature and purpose of the oral language to be promoted in the English classroom but, of equal importance, in his insistence that the purposes of writing are not solely a means of testing what has been learned, but a vital part of the process by which learning takes place. Kingman also emphasises the need for such knowledge, and Professor Cox takes it up again in his reports:

Structured and sensitive teaching is essential if children's development as writers is to thrive. . . . Good primary teachers pay attention to the process of writing, developed from knowledge and understanding of the practice of experienced writers (including themselves); they are then able to provide classroom practices which allow children to behave like real writers.[13]

The comment here is directly addressed to primary teachers, but the processes to which it refers are appropriate to all stages of learning. The particular value of Cox's advice, however, for the purposes of this study, lies in the sources to which he directs us in gaining knowledge and understanding of the writing process, since, in the context of poetry, the 'experienced writers' are, in this case, poets themselves. Their practice is evidenced, not only in the finished products of their poems, but in the wealth of commentary with which they provide us in their prose writing, both on the linguistic processes which they perceive to be the stages by which poetry comes into being, as well as what they have learned from their own mentors in their relationships with fellow poets in the community of artists, past and present, of which they are a part. All this is invaluable to teachers in informing their own approach to writing, for the practice of experienced poets contains much which could be described in the formulating processes outlined by Moffett or Bullock. In addition, the terminology which experienced writers use to define the territory in which their craft is learned and practised has much in common with the language of the workshop which describes to-day's English classrooms. The experience of real poets shows that their poems, like Bullock's 'knowledge', come into being as a result of a process which is worked out in the act of writing it, rather than in the simple transfer of it ready-made from the mind to the page. It is important that teachers are knowledgeable about these processes, first, if poetry writing is to be properly integrated into the learning experiences of the whole of the English curriculum and not to be the 'minor amenity' which Newsom saw it in danger of becoming, and, secondly, if they are to have the skills necessary to respond to pupils' poetry in ways which will help young writers to develop their writing ability beyond the expressive stages, which are, of course, central to the creative process. Andrew's enthusiasm about football, reflected in his expressive writing, was only the starting point in the process of learning how to write the instructions for playing it, but essential to his motivation.

A poem is both a 'thing made' and a 'thing said' and it is often supposed that it is the compulsion to *say* something of general significance to the reader which is the initial motivating force of poetry. But knowledge of the practice of real poets suggests that they more often see themselves as practitioners of a craft of making than as angels speaking to men. W. B. Yeats, more usually associated with the mysteries of a Romantic view of poetry, urged would-be poets in Ireland to 'learn your trade' and to celebrate or sing only 'whatever is well made' in their writing.[14] Seamus Heaney is another more recent example: a poet who makes a close identification between the occupation of the poet and the rural trades of Ireland in his poetry, seeing the learning of craft, together, of course, with gifts which cannot be learned – the 'watermarking of your essential patterns of perception' – as the major preoccupation of the poet. The combination of these is, for Heaney, a marriage of craft and technique in the acquisition of the poet's voice:

Craft is the skill of making. . . . Technique is what turns, in Yeats's phrase, 'the bundle of accident and incoherence that sits down to breakfast' into 'an idea, something intended, complete'.[15]

Craft is what the apprentice poet learns from the master craftsmen. Technique is, in Heaney's terms, the 'creative effort of the mind's and body's resources to bring the meaning of experience within the jurisdiction of form'.[16] But how does a poet begin to learn this craft, and how can the teacher help young apprentices – the bundles of accident and incoherence which sit down in the English workshop – to learn the technique of bringing their experience into the 'jurisdiction of form'?

Wordsworth gives some indication of the answer to this question by pointing to the 'hiding places' of his art. Describing the genesis of his long poem 'The Thorn', in a letter written to Isabella Fenwick in 1843, he claims that the poem was suggested to him by the sight of an old, stunted thorn-tree on the ridge of the Quantock Hills. The poem, he says,

. . . arose out of my observing on the ridge of Quantock Hills, on a stormy day, a thorn which I had often passed in calm and bright weather without noticing it. I said to myself, 'Cannot I by some invention do as much to make this thorn permanently an impressive object, as the storm has made it to my eyes at this moment'? I began the poem accordingly, and composed it with great rapidity.[17]

Wordsworth's poem begins with reflection and *observation,* and his first urge is to record, to make permanent the object observed. But in the process of doing so, the poem grows and becomes something else; in what Heaney calls the 'magnetic power' of 'a field of force',[18] the original observation gains resonances from the memory of the ballad of Martha Ray by which it is fertilised. Buffeted by the storm and the cruel forces of nature, the image of the thorn is forced into the attention of the observer in new ways, so that it comes to objectify, not just the tragic experience of Martha Ray, the woman who kills her illegitimate baby and buries it, but all the helpless sufferings of mankind, bent to breaking by forces in nature against which it is powerless. The process in the making of this remarkable poem is a sequence from observation of the particular to the universal perceptions about life and nature to which it leads: the thorn tree and the little hill of moss which surrounds it an occasion for the poet's reflection on an old ballad and a symbol for all those forces in nature which hurt and heal. The point to be made here is that Wordsworth's initial impulse is not to *say* something about those great and universal issues, but to *make* something out of what he has seen. The final poem is found in the process of carrying out an intention which was 'altered in fulfilment' as T. S. Eliot put it, describing a similar process of discovery in the journey of his own personal and poetic explorations:

> . . . And what you thought you came for
> Is only a shell, a husk of meaning
> From which the purpose breaks only when it is fulfilled
> If at all. Either you had no purpose
> Or the purpose is beyond the end you figured
> And is altered in fulfilment.[19]

Seamus Heaney says that, for him, it is difficult to discriminate between 'feeling getting into words' and 'words turning into feeling',[20] an indication, not just of the interrelated nature of his own definitions of 'craft', 'technique' and 'gift', but of the same formulating processes which Eliot had in mind when he wrote about his anxieties concerning the state of what he called 'literacy' among poets of his time:

What would make me most apprehensive about the future of the language and that implies the future of sensibility – or what we cease to be able to find words for, we cease to be able to feel – would be to observe a decreasing level of literacy among poets.[21]

What both poets are suggesting here is that to bring poetry into being is, like Bullock's belief in relation to knowledge, also a formulating process, in which words generate feeling as surely as feeling also determines the jurisdiction of form. It is this knowledge – of the interpenetration of language and experience – which poets demonstrate in their practice and which teachers, too, must understand if they are to increase the level of 'literacy' among the poets in their classrooms. Interestingly, D. W. Harding, in the Sixties, clearly understood it too when he wrote:

. . . if we manage to convey experiences precisely, that may be due partly to the fact that available modes of expression were influencing the experience from the start.[22]

The first lesson then in the application of such knowledge to the learning processes of apprentice writers – both teachers and pupils – is the need to learn how to observe and to find from their language resources words to record their observations, for it is this first step on the language 'ladder' from which all poets go on to develop their craft. This was part of the lesson of 'North', already referred to in the previous chapter, which Seamus Heaney acquired in the process of listening to the 'ocean-deafened' voices of the Viking invaders from Ireland's violent history and the 'swimming tongue' of their longship:

> It said, ' Lie down
> in the word-hoard, burrow
> the coil and gleam
> of your furrowed brain.
>
> .   .   .   .
>
> Keep your eye clear
> as the bleb of the icicle,
> trust the feel of what nubbed treasure
> your hands have known.' [23]

For Heaney, the observation, recorded as a result of his clarity of vision, is transformed, like Wordsworth's thorn, into the image through which his explorations into the nature of personal and national experience become the embodied truths of his major poetry. The initial finding of a poetic 'voice' is, for Heaney, as for all poets, the discovery of image: the language of metaphor crafted from the world of observation.

What the teacher can learn from this – particularly the teacher at primary level whose job it is to teach many subjects – is that the whole curriculum becomes a context for the teaching of observation and hence, potentially, for the discovery of the 'hiding places' of the 'nubbed treasure' poetry. Here is an example. A group of very young children were looking at shells and sea creatures as part of a project in

which they were investigating the sea. Their observations were recorded by the teacher on the chalkboard:

> Jellyfish
> Six inches broad
> Round, like a bell,
> Fringed with threads
> Stinging mouth
> Pink and grey
> Wobbly, soft
> Like jelly
> Fish jelly
> Jelly fish.

The notes already begin to take on the shape of a poem and the
'seeing' might seem clear enough here, but could it be made even
more precise? T. E. Hulme, not himself a major poet, but the
aesthetician and philosopher who brought a number of 'apprentice'
poets together in the Poets' Club which he founded in 1908, and
which went on to form one of the most significant movements in
modern English poetry, Imagism and hence Modernism, had this to
say about observation:

The straightforward use of words always lets the individuality of things
escape. Language, being a communal apparatus, only conveys over that
part of the emotion that is common to all of us. If you are able to
observe the actual individuality of the emotion you experience, you become dissatisfied with language. You persist in an endeavour to so state
things that the meaning does not escape, but is definitely forced on the
attention of the reader. . . . It is because language will not carry over the
exact thing you want to say, that you are compelled simply, in order to
be accurate, to invent original ways of stating things.[24]

'Ordinary' language – for Hulme, the straightforward use of words,
language as it is used in the transactions of everyday life – only expresses the stereotyped or the general perception. For example, we
say, 'I love John, I love holidays, I love ghost stories', 'The carpet is

red', 'Roses are red', 'Her face is red', 'Red is a colour', etc. In order to distinguish between different kinds of love or different kinds of red, Hulme suggests that the poet has to struggle with his medium, language, and invent original ways of defining the individuality of the things he sees and feels. For Hulme, and more importantly for his pupils and those to follow – the Modernists, Eliot, Pound and Joyce – these new ways of stating things crystallised in the Image: a metaphoric language, not used (as some pupils and teachers often mistakenly believe) in order to 'dress up' ordinary language to make it look more 'poetic', but in the greater interest of exactitude and precision.

Such understanding of the need for metaphor in the processes of seeing is exemplified in the poem which follows. The P2 pupils were encouraged by their teacher to look more precisely at the shapes of things around them in their investigation of the sea. Since the purpose is first to observe, the teacher directed the form of the poem by using the word 'starfish' as the initial letter of each line:

Shells-homes for creatures, hard fragile-breakable
tentacles-sticking up arms, bending from side to side
antennae-helping to breathe suck and feel tunneller take care!
razor fish-long sharp cutter sand

fish-shark - teeth, sharp and jagged
I wouldnt like to meet you tongue a red carpet!
Scallop-fan shaped surface of the moon, food-dish, soap dish

hermit crab-big ugly house-mover!

What is remarkable about this writing is that the knowledge learned about the sea creatures – the use of antennae, for example – is combined with close observation of the shape and feel of the shells, 'scallop-fan-shaped surface of the moon', to produce an exact image, of the kind defined by Hulme, of the total experience. In addition, these very young pupils are learning about the real use of metaphor and image in poetry. This was a class poem, of course, to which everyone contributed as the teacher made the notes on the board.

It is easy to see how, at a later stage, pupils can begin to make their own notes from such observations and begin to draft. Here a P7 girl is looking at derelict buildings in a street due for demolition near her school:

Dingy, dirty houses. Bricks falling out of walls, bricked up windows of ugly concrete. Writing on the walls, political slogans chalked on doors. Beer cans, plastic trays from carry-outs, broken bottles. Rubbish everywhere.

At this point the teacher talks to the class about how to look at old buildings and disused houses. They read the following: the first, an Imagist poem by T. E. Hulme, the second, an extract from the first part of T. S. Eliot's long poem, 'East Coker':

> Old houses were scaffolding once
> And workmen whistling.[25]

> In succession
> Houses rise and fall, crumble, are extended
> Are removed, destroyed, restored, or in their place
> Is an open field, or a factory, or a by-pass.
> Old stone to new building, old timber to new fires
> Old fires to ashes and ashes to the earth
>
> . . . .
> Houses live and die [26]

Both poems observe accurately, recording the passing of time as houses, like people, live and die. Both use personification, the first image identifying the excitement of the new building with whistling workmen, the second the life cycle itself as the old gives way to the new – a familiar part of any urban landscape. In both poems, the 'thing made' in the image of the poem starts to assume greater importance as a 'thing said' where the literal world of observation – the men on the scaffolding or the urban by-pass – comes to stand for every-

thing that is transient in life, human and natural. Could the same
technique help the girl with her poem? In the poem which follows,
the young apprentice is attempting her own tentative 'inventions'
from what she has learned about personification:

> The old house sags at its shoulders like a tired man,
> Blind eyes stare vacantly from empty windows.
> Rain on pavement's chalk-designs make colours run
> Like eye shadow on sad ladies' faces.

Learning something of this process offers the same challenge to
teachers. The following extracts are taken from poems written by a
group of teachers during a course on poetry which they took as part
of a post-graduate programme. They were observing the environment in which they were being taught and the journey which they
made each Wednesday in the dark days of February, for most, after a
hard day's teaching, regularly passing the same landmarks as they made
their way down a long corridor to the tutor's room:

> There's Eric and Jack,
> Proud sentinels –
> Coffee mugs, familiar nods,
> And still no one wants to play badminton.
>
> > *Damian*

> Six-fifteen on Wednesday night,
> Coffee cups drained,
> Bulging bookshelves, prints, figweeps.
> Fragments of Eliot, Heaney digging
> Capturing the moment.
>
> > *Mary*

> Leaving school the traffic subsides for a while
> Like the cries of children.
> Thoughts thin to irrelevant ponderings
> Shrugging off

Dull responsibilities
Repetitious routine.
Cats' eyes blink distractedly as darkness
Blackens my mind.
A dull rhythm reverberates from a neighbouring car,
Windows wound down slightly
Clearing misted windscreens,
Restoring vision once more.

Lorraine

The tutor speaks with a slow voice
Energetic words
The tortoise and the hare
in one.

Clare

These are accurate observations, all conveying a record of personal experience: the porters (Jack and Eric), the notice board with the invitation to students to join the badminton club, the dying plant, the voice of the tutor, along with all the sounds and sights of the journey itself. Through these, the writers convey something of their individual perceptions of the experience: the blinking of the cats' eyes in the darkness and the failure of the advertisement to attract customers, for example, say something about the sense of bewildered anxiety of writers as they face the unknown 'darkness' of what lies ahead and the inevitable feeling surrounding the monotonous recurrence of doing the same journey week after week. In the example which follows, such observation becomes the sustained image of the whole poem:

On each attentive ear fall her slow, soft vowels,
Tentatively teasing out our halting clumsy responses,
She patiently threads her way
Through the silence of our
Inadequacy.
Outside, the early winter green of the cherry
Struggles to calm its vigorous impulse
Prematurely to unfurl its white confetti.

Inside, we slowly make our way through metaphor and symbol,
Faltering in the greyness of the twilight hour,
We launch our apprehensive search
Through the terrain of words,
Landscaped with love's labour by the poet and craftsman.
Here we dig over their symbolic patterns,
Delving each deep furrow,
Harvesting the crafted image.
Each reader's liberated consciousness,
A glimpsed discovery of poetry and the poet's vocation.
Outside, the white spray of the cherry tree,
Bursting from its darkness,
Initiates a solemn moment of its own fulfilment.

Eileen

Eileen is here, like the others, recording the impressions which surround her: the bare cherry tree, observed from the window, conveying, as other images from the poems quoted above, a similar sense of time passing from week to week. But in the image of blossoming at the end of her poem, there is not only the moment of fulfilment and achievement of the tree, but the survival and fulfilment of the writer whose responses to the poetry she has studied have blossomed as well. This is not stated, of course, but for her, as for Ezra Pound, the Imagist, 'The image itself is the speech. The image is the word beyond formulated language'.[27] In this poem, the 'thing made' and the 'thing said' are one.

In all these examples, writers are discovering how image works in poetry, and because they are able to observe the actual individuality of the emotions they are experiencing, they are, as Hulme suggested, dissatisfied with 'ordinary' language, finding instead from the world of their actual experience, 'original ways of stating things'. It is often supposed that this is the work of the imagination in creative effort, but 'imagination' is both a misunderstood and much over-used word. Pupils are constantly asked to 'use your imagination' or 'use lots and lots of descriptive words', and the idea which many of them have about what they are expected to do is to conjure up some fantasy world; the more devoid it is of reality, the more 'imaginative' it is.

Imagination, however, like speculation, is based on knowledge and experience. Blake's imaginative 'tyger' – a creature of his own creation, belonging to the forests of mental darkness rather than some earthly jungle – has not lost touch with the observable world of cats, just as, on another level, the marvellous fantasy world of E. B. White's *Charlotte's Web*, the story of a superior spider, Charlotte, who makes friends with the pig, Wilbur, in Zuchermann's barn, belongs to the real world of spiders. Charlotte can speak and spell and she tells Wilbur precisely how she spins her web and why, just as Wilbur's idea of a gourmet feast is properly and appropriately for him the delights of pig-swill: potato peels and left-over vegetables. The speculative world of the imagination is only convincing and 'real' when it is based on close observation. In the example which follows, the progression from observation to spectulation is worked out. Here a boy describes an old man he sees regularly in church:

He sits in front of us in Church every Sunday. His glasses leave marks on the sides of his swollen red face, when he takes them off to wipe his eyes with his handkerchief. When we say our prayers, he always says 'Amen' after everybody else has sat up. He falls asleep in the middle of the sermon and you can sometimes hear him snoring quietly as his head falls forward. He always lifts his hat to us and says 'Nice day' as he limps off down the street on his stick.

And here the poet, Philip Larkin, imagines and speculates about what it is like to be old:

> Perhaps being old is having lighted rooms
> Inside your head, and people in them, acting.
> People you know, yet can't quite name; each looms
> Like a deep loss restored, from known doors turning,
> Setting down a lamp, smiling from a stair, extracting
> A known book from the shelves; or sometimes only
> The rooms themselves, chairs and a fire burning,
> The blown bush at the window, or the sun's
> Faint friendliness on the wall some lonely,
> Rain-ceased mid-summer evening. That is where they live:
> Not here and now, but where all happened once.[28]

This is not generalised language about the old, but a series of precise images in which the more real world of memory which they inhabit is encapsulated and lived. The boy 'imagines' likewise:

MY GRANNY

> My Granny stumps about on swollen legs,
> Kind eyes hidden in her wrinkled face,
> Her arms outstretched to hug and hold.
> But underneath her smiles I think she's sad.
> She quarrels with my Mum about my Dad,
> And then alone,
> In her big chair upstairs,
> Her worried lines relax
> And dreams comes back
> Of her lost son, a boy like me.
>
> *Robert P5*

This, like the other examples of pupils' work, shows how the 'reception' of poets' techniques as well as their language, allow the individual greater possibility for imagining and hence for greater 'production of language'.

Poetry, as the Northern Ireland report rightly stressed, is important because of the quality of the language at work on experience which it offers us. Essentially, that quality is the degree of precision and accuracy which it achieves in remaking experience in all its individuality: its colour, shape and sound, together with the emotions and feelings which it generates. It is this same quality which poets admire in one another's work, as all the 'manifestoes' which have marked major periods of innovation throughout the history of poetry demonstrate. It is important, therefore, that pupils are taught how to appreciate this quality and, as the P2 poem shows, this can be achieved even from the earliest age. (Pleasure in the sound of words which match or correspond exactly to the experience to be conveyed is another example: slippery, shiny worm, buzzing bees, etc.) One way to encourage this critical sense is to introduce poems written by experienced poets to set beside and compare with the pupils' own. For example, a selection of poems was put together to be used with groups of pupils from P2-P7 from a variety of schools set both in urban areas and in different parts of the County Down coast. The poems chosen – or sometimes extracts from longer poems – focussed roughly on the theme of the street in an attempt to find a common experience of the home/school environment on which the pupils would eventually write. The object was that pupils would share their poems among the schools involved in the project, thereby enlarging the 'audience' for the writing outside the classroom itself. The selection included the first of T. S. Eliot's 'Preludes', a street observed at six o'clock in the evening, some of Douglas Dunn's Terry Street poems about Glasgow, some single-image poems of the Imagist-type, like the T. E. Hulme poem already referred to, and a selection of writing by children. The collection amounted to some twenty-five poems. The following are two examples:

PRELUDES

The winter evening settles down
With smell of steaks in passage ways.
Six o'clock.
The burnt-out ends of smoky days.
And now a gusty shower wraps
The grimy scraps
Of withered leaves about your feet
And newspapers from vacant lots;
The showers beat
On broken bricks and chimney-pots,
And at the corner of the street
A lonely cab-horse steams and stamps.

And then the lighting of the lamps.[29]

OUR STREET AT NIGHT

Night time falls over our street
The lamps shine down on the red brick houses
One or two weary workers clomp home
From a hard days work.
The blinds are down over the windows
At the co-op across the road.
From the fish-shop a delicious smell
Steals out into the night air.
David is crying
He has to go into bed.
A few cats stealthily prowl around.
Bim, an ancient mongrel dog,
Scratches the house door
Asking to be let in.
Whispy smoke rises
From the chimneys
As the night fires are lit.
There's Mrs B . . .
Drawing her curtains
And turning her living room light on.
Suddenly the night silence is shattered
When Mr S . . . booms off to work
On his blooming motor bike.
He works on the night shift
At Ardsley pit.
On push bikes,
Motor bikes,
In cars,
Or just walking
The youth group set out for home.
The silence falls
And it is as if our street
Has fallen asleep.

Boy aged 10 [30]

Pupils were asked to pick out the sights, sounds and smells of both poems and to find differences. In particular, they looked at the Eliot image 'The burnt-out ends of smoky days' and worked out how a day could be burnt-out like a thrown-away cigarette-end, perhaps. They speculated about what kind of a street this was, concluding that the boy's street was busier, noisier and perhaps, too, a happier place to live in than Eliot's dingy, lonely street where everything seemed useless and finished. From there, they went on to work out how the images we choose to record our observations can convey what we feel about things. They compared the two fog image-poems also included in the selection:

FOG (I)

The fog smothers the town
Like a rug of fur
It cuddles round people
Like a hand of wool

Robert, P4

FOG (II)

The fog curls itself around the house
It slithers across roof-tops like a snake after its prey.
It looks for smoke to make itself
Larger, thicker and deadlier

David, P4

Both poets are looking at fog, each seeing it differently, Robert finding it cosy and friendly, David, on the other hand, sinister and threatening. Some volunteered the view that 'smothers' in Fog (I) was good but 'a hand of wool' was 'over the top'! Robert wasn't really thinking clearly about fog, only trying to be clever, one thought. Others disagreed, so they went on to experiment with images of their own, reading the Eliot passage from 'The Love Song of J. Alfred Prufrock' which compares fog with a cat, to add to their verbal resources. The writing which followed revealed a mixed response. Some children were able, in their own writing, only to repeat the images they had heard and read: an instance here where limited reception of language can actually inhibit the possibilities for further production of language. But all the pupils got the idea and worked hard at observing the individuality of their own environment. One P5 girl in a composite P4/P5 class in Newcastle, County Down, who had had little experience of writing poetry, produced the lines:

> The winter evening settles down
> In his big armchair outside our town
> He makes the trees sway back and forth
> As if they were going to fall.
>
> *Leonna, P5*

Leonna had seen the metaphor in Eliot's use of 'settles down' in his first line and had extended it to produce a nice – and an accurate – image of her own. Here is another example from the same class which, with its catalogue of names and happenings, is Helen's version of a similar technique used by Dylan Thomas in *Under Milk Wood* :

MY STREET

> There's Dympna Cunningham craning her ears,
> There's Helena Wallace trying to soothe her baby,
> The diggers, the diggers are making a row!
> Get off the road, the diggers are coming!
> Bikes race off the road,
> Children give a piercing cry and scatter,
> The diggers rumble past,
> Dympna Cunningham takes her hands from her ears,
> Helena Wallace's baby stops crying,
> Till the next digger comes by.
>
> *Helen, P4*

Another group, this time of P6 children in Portaferry, County Down, in a lovely school overlooking Strangford Lough, talked about their street in the light of the poems they had read. Portaferry is unique, because it has a ferry which sails from their village to Strangford on the opposite shore. They thought about the word 'sails': this was

what T. E. Hulme would have called 'ordinary' language, the generalised word we use for ships – like yachts, or liners, or tall ships. Did
their ferry sail? They laughed. No, it 'beat' the water, it 'chugged', it
'thumped', it 'cut' and 'bumped'. And the seagulls? Birds 'sing'. Did
seagulls sing? No, they laughed. They screech and scold. So they
tried to find words to describe the sounds to be heard in Portaferry in
the evening. One quiet boy who had not said anything suggested
that if you listened really carefully you could hear 'the crabs crackling
under the bricks' and explained to the puzzled teacher that the crabs
came in at night when the tide went out to shelter along the back of
the harbour wall and that you could sometimes hear them if you
knew when to listen. This was certainly an observation special to
Portaferry, and sharing it later with pupils from Bangor, the crabs of
the real experience of one poet became the imagined image of others:

TWILIGHT IN BANGOR

Dusk falls over Bangor
Waves lap upon the shore;
The rumble of the Crawfordsburn train heard in the
distance,
Like some huge, angry, prowling animal.
A light film of mist falls across the bay,
A lonely crab scuttles out on the sand,
A few gulls wheel above squawking
Like banshees,
As the fishing trawlers drift in.
                                    Joanne, P6

BANGOR BAY

Sea is a monster
A fearless terrible monster,
Snarling, swallowing sand and shingle,
Splashing, pounding ships in harbour.
Sheltering crabs

Scuttle to and fro;
White horses ride the
Waves in Bangor Bay.

Michael, P6

Here apprentices to the trade of writing are learning from one another, readers in one school illustrating how pupils amass a store of images from half-remembered poems, of lines from plays, of phrases, rhythms and ideas, as Kingman had pointed out they should, from the wide range of literature they are experiencing; and how, once again, such reception of language enables the writer to 'use his imagination' by experimentation with his resources in a new context.

Such reception of language is obviously not confined to poetry but, as the Kingman comment indicates, is inclusive of wide reading from literature in general, as indeed from all aspects of the curriculum, where understanding and knowledge about language can be stimulated. The more conscious sense in which the cultural heritage of Ireland is to be more explicit in the curriculum can only further increase and heighten appreciation of the environment and sharpen the eye of the observer to the 'nubbed treasures' which are to everyone's hands in the landscape which surrounds us. The group of P4/ P5 pupils from Newcastle, whose work has already been referred to, went on from their 'street' poems to look at the Mourne mountains from their school yard which literally adjoins the foothills of Slieve Donard. They had a good knowledge of the geography of the place and they had been reading some of the myths and legends from their Irish heritage. These are some of the poems which combine observation and speculation in quite remarkable writing:

THE VIEW FROM OUR SCHOOL

Standing in the playground
I can see Slieve Donard, the mountain,
With Thomas his son.
Just near, the valley Blackstairs is flowing.
Every time I see the Saddle

I wonder if it gets its name from Finn McCool.
Did he ride the mountains like a horse
And flatten out that valley in between?
Up from the Saddle is Mummy Commedagh,
Swooping down to meet Slieve Donard.
There they stand, hand in hand,
Looking down over the school.

Siobhan, P4

THE MOUNTAINS OF MOURNE IN WINTER

Slieve Donard's a giant with snow on his head,
Beside little Thomas with no snow at all,
And the Blackstairs frozen stiff.
There is Commedagh with plenty of snow
And Drumakilly with trees of rust and green.
As the sun moves, the shadows come and go,
The quarry is gleaming and glooming.
Bang! – there goes an explosion,
See the dust and a puff of smoke,
(For men need granite to make our footpaths.)
Between Commedagh and Donard
A valley lies.
It's called the saddle
Can you guess why?

Clare, P4

In these poems, cultural heritage – the legends of Finn McCool
and knowledge of local place names – become part of the word-
hoard of the class, brought in to focus attention on the particular
and to convey exactly what they saw in their mountain and their
speculation about its history. This class had no difficulty manipulating terms like personification, image and imagination, and
discussed the poems they had written, using these terms quite
naturally. The example, quoted also in the last chapter, leaves
little more to be said about the clear 'bleb of the icicle' of the eye
of this young writer or about poetry and cross-curricularity:

OUR SCHOOL YARD

Black-headed gulls come every day
To our school yard.
They're our dustmen,
For they pick up all our rubbish.
Their uniform is not green like ours –
It's white with a dark brown cap.
But in winter they leave off their caps
     Silly birds!
And wear their Walkmans instead.

Roisin, P5

The Cox Report on the Programmes of Study for England and Wales emphasised, as Bullock had before, the need to ensure a sense of progression in English. One of the problems of much of the 'creative writing' approach of the Sixties and since was that progression was often not planned for, the assumption being that pupils would make progress simply by repeating poetry writing. This is not necessarily the case, however, particularly for reluctant writers who feel little more than frustration when they are confronted with the demands to write yet another poem, with little indication from the teacher about how to do it better, apart from the encouraging comment, 'Quite good', 'Fair', 'Keep trying', hurriedly written at the bottom. Assessment is difficult where poetry is concerned and it would be utterly at variance with the principles on which the writing workshop is based to adopt what Andrew Wilkinson described as the role of 'the teacher as self-appointed proof reader . . . GRowling and SPitting and hiSSing from the margin.'[31]

How then are teachers to be encouraging and at the same time ensure that their apprentices learn from one attempt to another? Cox speaks of the need for pupils to read their writing 'as if they were in the intended reader's place, and to revise, redraft and proof-read their work with the reader in mind.'[32] In such a way, they learn to create, polish and produce (individually or collaboratively) extended written texts. This is one way in which to ensure the 'articulated progression'

Geoffrey Summerfield suggested as an alternative to the 'chronic non-co-ordination of learning and a non-policy of *ad hoc* excitements' of the Sixties.[33] The Northern Ireland Report, like the Cox Report, rightly suggests that in the context of ensuring progression within the writing task, the conventions of spelling, punctuation and syntax are best learned in the context of pupils' own writing and in the re-drafting processes. But there is more to revising and editing than what the Northern Ireland paper refers to as 'secretarial skills',[34] however important these are. There is also compositional redrafting, that is, making amendments to a text in the interests of more effective communication with the audience for whom it is intended – or indeed simply to make the writing 'better', (more 'accurate' in Hulme's sense of the term) for its own sake. Pupils, and teachers too, are surprised when they see the drafting processes which 'real' and experienced poets undertake. A look, for example, at the genesis of Seamus Heaney's poem 'North' shows that he attempted six different drafts before he arrived at the final version, the title itself changing from 'North Atlantic', 'Northerners', and finally to 'North' as the work progressed.[35] Words and phrases are changed, crossed out, circled and replaced as the poem alters in the fulfilment of its making. T. S. Eliot's long poem, *The Waste Land* underwent such radical revision, both by the poet himself and by Ezra Pound, the poet 'teacher' to whom Eliot dedicated the poem, addressing him in his epitaph as 'il miglior fabbro', the better craftsman, that the final published poem is only half the length of the original version.[36] While pupils obviously could not actually read and study such manuscripts, they are astonished when they are shown the densely annotated facsimile and their responses are almost always the same: 'Oh dear, he made an awful lot of mistakes didn't he?' (an indication too, of their perceptions of 'right' and 'wrong' in the writing context). Too often, of course, pupils are expected to write – often mistakenly, too, under a 'given' title – and to get it 'right' first time. Indeed, many are reluctant in discussing their work with even a sympathetic and appreciative audience, to cross out words and spoil the pristine condition of the page. But learning to do this is to behave like real writers and, in the process, what is gained is invaluable as pupils become more closely involved in independent self-assessment and learn critical skills which enable them to progress, not just within a single text, but from one writing activity to another.

T. S. Eliot's practice in his revision of *The Waste Land* illustrates the process well, as do the intervention and collaboration of 'il miglior fabbro', though there is much GRowling, SPitting and hiSSing in the margins of the manuscripts as well which showed that Pound had not enough of the patience of the good classroom practitioner! Ezra Pound, like T. E. Hulme, was much concerned with accuracy in language and image and believed, from his reading of Ernest Fenollosa's essay, 'The Chinese Written Character as a Medium for Poetry', that the ideogram was a more exact form of language than the abstractions to which European languages tended. Ask a European, Pound said, 'What is red?' and he will answer, 'Red is a colour', where the Chinese, on the other hand, will define red by giving you abbreviated pictures of red things: rose, iron rust, cherry, flamingo. In Chinese, neither a pure noun nor pure verb exists. Things are only the terminal points of actions. Abstract verbs are not possible in nature. For example, 'spring' is an ideogram showing the sun underlying the bursting forth of plants, 'east' is a picture of the sun sign tangled in the branches of the tree sign: in each, the eye sees noun and verb as one.[37] Consequently, much of Eliot's revision was directed at replacing abstract or generalised language by concrete images of this kind. One example from the manuscripts will illustrate the process. The whole of *The Waste Land* is a marvellous example of how reception of other poets' language allowed Eliot not just greater possibility for the production of his own images, but to show how knowledge of the wider cultural heritage of European Literature, world religions and the anthropological myths on which the poem is based, extends the poem's meaning from the initial world of his observation to the universal. In this example, the poet borrows lines from Goldsmith's, *The Vicar of Wakefield*:

> When lovely woman stoops to folly
> And finds too late that men betray,
> What charms can soothe her melancholy?
> What art can wash her tears away?

Eliot changes these lines, so that, in his revised text, they become:

> When lovely woman stoops to folly and
> Paces about the room again, alone,
> She smoothes her hair with automatic hand,
> And puts a record on the gramophone.

Here the vagueness of the abstract and generalised questions 'What charms . . . ?', 'What art . . . ?' are replaced by the negative answers which, in Eliot's context of waste and emptiness, must answer them: pacing about the room, putting a record on the gramophone, are dramatic images of inaction which suggest little more than a helpless return to the routines of the day.[38]

Pupils' revisions are, in the first instance, attempts of a similar sort: looking at the generalised, abstract and 'ordinary' words to see if a more concrete image might replace them. The following extract demonstrates the process at work in the classroom:

DRAFT 1

> The *sound* of waves on the shore
> Water *coming up and down* the beach
> Gulls *flying* in the wind.

'Sound', 'coming up and down', 'flying' are all abstract words which let the 'individuality of things escape', as T. E. Hulme might have said. Concerned to convey the actual sound of the waves, the girl crosses 'sound' out and tries 'smash', then goes on to experiment with rhyme to combine the sounds of water with the action of the tide on the shingled beach. Gulls 'flying' in the wind is a reworked image which extends the suggestion of the hand of the water to the hands of the wind in her revised version and suggests something of the help-lessness of things against the greater forces of nature. This is not quite Wordsworthian, but she is clearly thinking beyond the particular observation to reflect on the more cruel forces implicit in the action of the wind:

DRAFT 2

Sudden smash of waves on land
Grasps shingle
Rasps in receding water
Screeching gulls
Driven in the hands of the wind
To remote corners of the sky.

This is one sort of revision and there are, of course, others, where the use of the computer can help in experimenting with varying lengths of line, for example, in attempting different forms and poem shapes. Consideration of an audience from another school, perhaps, where the readership is extended to include pupils from schools outside Northern Ireland, might require the provision of additional information given in a glossary to help them to respond to particular kinds of writing where, for example, dialect words are deliberately used in place of the standard form. Lucy Calkins, in *Lessons from a Child*,[39] includes an account of the processes of writing and revision which suggest an audience of another sort, however. Susie is here describing to her friend how she came to write her poem:

One day me and my father took a walk in the woods. It was dim and our shoes made little balls of ice that went rolling down the hill.

And so she drafts her poem:

DRAFT 1

The sun shone down low in the sky.
Tiny snowballs, making go downhill.
Sun, Beautiful, beyond hill
Warm crisp air. My Father: wonderful,
Nice. Liking, like me, the best
Mine. Brightness, beauty, trees
Peace all around.

. . . 'Some of this they may not understand . . . the part about my father liking, like me'.

. . . 'I'm trying to think of a special word for my dad. He's not like any other person . . . '

'You can write a poem saying about things, you can tell about the feelings. But, like, the poem has to *be* the feelings, not just tell them'.

She tries again:

DRAFT 2

THE WONDERFUL WALK

Walking through the woods
Dad and I.
Not worrying,
Not today.
Not talking of troubles but of
Smooth soft sparkling snow
And bright sun going down
Sharing the beauty
The Wonderful Walk.

Diane praises it: '*Final!* . . . I *love* it'. But Susie replies:
I'm not sure I'm getting the exact feelings I'm trying to get . . . how clean, how white, and the sun shining. How good we felt!?

The interesting question at this stage of the revision is not which the better version of Susie's poem is, but for whom she is actually writing. The approval of her friend is clearly not enough for her. Philip Larkin throws interesting light on Susie's impulse and her audience in describing his own:

I write poems to preserve things I have seen/thought/felt (if I may so indicate a composite and complex experience) both for myself and for others, though I feel that my prime responsibility is to the experience itself, which I am trying to keep from oblivion for its own sake. Why I should do this I have no idea, but I think the impulse to preserve lies at the bottom of all art.[40]

Susie's experience, like Wordsworth's sighting of the thorn-tree, or Larkin's poems, which preserve his experiences of the old or the young, observed from the corner of a railway carriage on a journey from Hull where he lived, to London, demonstrates that each wants to make permanent the 'impressive object' of experience, as Wordsworth put it. Their final responsibility is not to tell their audience about their experience, but so to remake it in the form and image of poetry that the poem itself becomes the experience: an independent, autonomous world of art where, by manipulation of language, evenings can settle down in armchairs, birds wear walkmans, giants make mountains, or the lonely crabs of the imagination scuttle under bricks for shelter. And it is in this that poetry finds its ultimate audience and purpose: the audience beyond self and others, where the motivation of the writer in the exercise of his craft is simply the pleasure of doing it.

[1] *Proposals for the English Curriculum.* Report of the English Working Group (Belfast: NICC, 1989), Chapter 2, 3.12, p.14.

[2] *Report of the Committee of Inquiry into the Teaching of English Language,* [the Kingman Report]. Department of Education and Science (London: HMSO, 1989), Chapter 2:21, quoted in *Proposals for the English Curriculum,* Chapter 2, 3.9, p.13.

[3] *ibid.,* Chapter 5, 1:15,16, p.59.

[4] *ibid.,* p.14.

[5] Geoffrey Summerfield, 'Great Expectations', *New Education,* Vol. 2, No. 3, March 1966.

[6] *Proposals for the English Curriculum.* Chapter 2, 2.5, p.6.

[7] *ibid.,* 1.3, p.4.

[8] *English from 5 to 16. Curriculum Matters 1.* Department of Education and Science (London: HMSO, 1984).

9   The best known of these were the *Breakthrough to Literacy* materials for young learners and P. S. Doughty and J. J. Pearce, *Language in Use* for older pupils.

10   J. C. Moffett, *Teaching the Universe of Discourse* (Boston: Houghton Mifflin 1968).

11   This example is taken from Andrew Wilkinson, et al., *Assessing Language Development* (Oxford: Oxford University Press,1980), pp.98,99.

12   *A Language for Life* [the Bullock Report]. Report of the Committee of Inquiry appointed by the Secretary of State for Education and Science (London: HMSO, 1975), 4.9, p.50.

13   *English for ages 5 to 11* [the first Cox Report]. Department of Education and Science (London: DES, 1988), Chapter 2.11, p.8.

14   W. B. Yeats, 'Under Ben Bulben', *Collected Poems* (London: Macmillan, 1967 edition), p.400.

15   Seamus Heaney, 'Feeling into Words', *Preoccupations: Selected Prose 1968-1978* (London: Faber, 1980), p.47.

16   *ibid.*

17   *Letters of William and Dorothy Wordsworth* (Oxford: Oxford University Press, 1937), quoted by Seamus Heaney, *Preoccupations,* p.50.

18   *ibid.,* p.51.

19   T. S. Eliot,'Little Gidding', *Collected Poems 1909-1962* (London: Faber, 1963), p.215.

20   *Preoccupations,* p.52.

21   T. S. Eliot, 'That Poetry is Made with Words', *New English Weekly,* xv, No. 2 (27 April, 1939).

22   D. W. Harding, 'Raids on the Inarticulate', *Use of English,* Vol. 19, No. 2 (Winter 1967).

23   'North', *North* (London: Faber 1975), pp.19, 20.

24   T. E. Hulme, *Speculations: Essays on Humanism and the Philosophy of Art,* edited by Herbert Read (London: K. Paul, Trench, Trubner, 1924), p.162.

25   T. E. Hulme, 'Images', *Imagist Poetry,* edited by Peter Jones (Harmondsworth: Penguin, 1972), p.49.

26   T. S. Eliot, 'East Coker', *Collected Poems,* p.196.

27   Ezra Pound,*Gaudier Brzeska: A Memoir* (London: Bodley Head,

1916), p.88.

28   Philip Larkin, 'The Old Fools', *High Windows* (London: Faber, 1974), pp.19,20.

29   T. S. Eliot, *Collected Poems*, p.23.

30   A. B. Clegg, *The Excitement of Writing* (London: Chatto and Windus,1964), p.48.

31   Anthony Adams and John Pearce, *Every English Teacher* (Oxford: Oxford University Press,1974), p.92, quoted in Brian Cox, *Cox on Cox: An English Curriculum for the 1990's* (London: Hodder and Stoughton, 1991), p.150.

32   *English for ages 5 to 11,* Chapter 10.33, p.52.

33   Geoffrey Summerfield, 'Great Expectations'. See p.39.

34   See *Proposals for the English Curriculum,* Chapter 5, passim.

35   Tony Curtis (editor), *The Art of Seamus Heaney* (Bridgend: Poetry Wales Press, 1985), pp.51-56 (not numbered).

36   T. S. Eliot, *The Waste Land: a Facsimile and Transcript of the Original Drafts,* edited by Valerie Eliot (London: Faber, 1971).

37   Gertrude Patterson, *T. S. Eliot: Poems in the Making* (Manchester: Manchester University Press, 1970), pp.64, 65.

38   *ibid.*, pp.69ff.

39   Lucy McCormick Calkins, *Lessons from a Child: On the Teaching and Learning of Writing* (Exeter, N.H.: Heinemann Educational, 1983), pp.140,141.

40   Philip Larkin, 'Statement', *Required Writing: Miscellaneous Pieces 1955-1982* (London: Faber,1983), p.79.

CHAPTER THREE

Clare Maloney

'In the saying and the doing'

An Exploration of the Teacher's and Learner's Experience of the Writing Process in the Primary Classroom.

IT WAS NOT MY ORIGINAL INTENTION to choose poetry as the subject of my Master's degree thesis. Indeed, the decision to take a poetry module was an impulsive one: a sudden desire to divert from the 'big-league' stuff of educational studies today – Management Theory, Curriculum Studies, Social Psychology and so on. As I began, therefore, what I had never intended to do, I did so with all the intrigue and trepidation of a volunteer from the audience approaching the stage.

On the very first night of that twelve-week poetry course, a welcome opportunity was offered to participants to introduce themselves and say something about why they were present. I listened with admiration as my fellow students spoke about on-going interests in poetry, an attraction to this or that poet. Always ready, like Heaney, to 'trust contrariness'[1] – often to the point of embodying it – I knew I could not claim any 'love' of poetry or any special interest in or familiarity with any particular poet. I could not pretend to be a reader of poetry and had only a vague memory of bits of Browning or Wordsworth which I had studied for my A-Levels. Indeed, as I admitted, rather tongue-in-cheek, the only reason I was there was because my attempt to reverse my original impulsive decision to do poetry had failed. Just before this first class had begun, I had tried to switch to a different module, but everything else was fully subscribed. Listening to my new classmates, my admiration for them set up a resonance with a growing suspicion. I sat back in my chair, 'surveying' their comments as though they were buns on a cake-stand. In the silence of my detached vantage point, I could detect the grand-mother-in-me whisper behind-hand to the mother-in-me, 'I'd say them's bought buns', to which came the reply, 'Sure you'd know to look at them!' Whether or not my suspicions were well-founded, the memory serves to illumine a subconscious, perhaps hereditary, attitude – similar indeed to that of many of the children I would later teach – which viewed poetry as a kind of fancy confectionery. Probing behind these inherited attitudes of mind, I began to wonder what the nature of 'home-made' poetry might be.

A clue to the nature of home-made poetry lay in the memory of one of my earliest experiences of poetry, an experience of 'names ... negotiation'[2] as Heaney might have called it. The first time I ever heard the word 'poetry', it slipped off my teacher's tongue like a dropped stitch from one of her knitting needles. I wasn't quite sure at the time whether she had said 'poetry' or 'poertry' (as Heaney also recalls in *Preoccupations*).[3] Being in P2 at the time, I considered myself a veteran of school. I had plotted and plumbed the socio-educational co-ordinates of the school world. I knew it all! Events like milk-time or home-time, giving out or collecting, telling tales or asking out to the toilet were all easy and familiar. In fact my only frustration was with the fat-leaded infant's pencil which I reckoned had about as much finesse as a thick lip and which slabbered letters on to my lovely clean pages where they lolled like disabled limbs. But 'poetry' or 'poertry' I had not heard of before. This word was new and I was curious. I ran my tongue over its contours as one would over the gap of a newly missing tooth. Poetry had an elegant, eloquent feel about it. It suggested the kind of cultured event in which the cup would be honoured with a saucer. It had the smooth, soft-vowelled texture of sifted flour or soda bread. 'Poertry' on the other hand, with its harshly consonanted 'r' suggested a more down-to-earth business, stone-ground flour or a wheaten farl.

Even as a young child, language – in this instance the word 'poetry' – had a physical feel to it. In the feel of it on one's tongue (perhaps the young child's most perceptive sense), one could distinguish between the crude and the refined, between the masculine and the feminine, perhaps eventually in a loose way between Romantic exuberance and the restraints of Classicism. The taste and feel for language – and especially for poetry – is gained through the senses. Words were 'verbal music' 'bedding the ear',[4] sucked through the tongue and rubbed-in with the tips of the fingers. It resides in such common-place as the formal ritual litany of the daily school roll-call; the solemn dignified tones of the Signing of the Cross; the elastication of one's name across the skin-tight light of the stretch-in-the-evenings as one is called in for bed; skipping rhymes whose metre is rendered visible in the turn of the rope like a revolving door, repeating its seductive invitation 'in'; the tap dance of feet on hopscotched paving slabs as one threads ones's way through squared, numbered stanzas, all the time negotiating a precarious balance between Classic stretch and Romantic reach of the imagination; the alla-balla alla-balla of a bouncing ball like one of the orbic disembodied pulses in Sean O'Riordain's poem 'Fiabhras',[5] the strict metric rule and form for counting playmates 'in' or 'out'; the pat-pat of a spade on an upturned bucket of sand accompanied by the appeasing incantation to the Gods of Creativity, 'Castle castle come out/And I'll give you a penny tomorrow'; the hands-on experience of creating unity of form in one perfect sandcastle and the equally valuable experience of many failures; the lined equidistance of running-a-pole and walking-a-pole, like pacing oneself over lines of poetry as opposed to paragraphs of prose and so on. Such experience and rituals are a raw, crude poetic 'praxis': a fusion in rhythm, of word and action, a fusion in the life of the child of language generating experience, and experience generating language.

Play constitutes much of the experience of young children. One might therefore rewrite the statement above, so that in the case of young children, it reads, – 'play generating experience and experience generating play', both of which 'interplay' with the child's development of language and language's development of the child. To illustrate the point, the two poems which follow were written by the teacher for her Junior Infant/P1 class. They are an attempt to offer the children an image of poetry and the process of poem-making, based on their own experience:

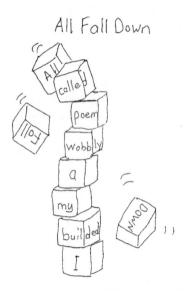

All Fall Down

Building on the idea of 'poetry as child's play' or, perhaps more accurately, building on the idea of the raw or crude material in the child's play as potential poetry, this poem plays on the fairly common image of words as building-blocks. It crudely constructs them into an appropriately 'wobbly' poem. The wobbly nature of the poem arises as much from the writer's uneasiness in playing with words and toying with poetry, in this childishly poetic way, as from the actual children's building of the blocks themselves. But play is the legitimate work of the infant classroom. And without a willingness on the part of the teacher to ' play around', the poem would not have been written. Infants whose teacher is not prepared to play are at a serious disadvantage in terms of their educational development. Infants whose teacher is not prepared to play with language, words and images, are at a serious disadvantage in terms of their linguistic development, not to mention the development of the teacher herself. Words and image are the literal building blocks of this poem; play is the process by which this poem was made. The poem represents the young child's experience *literally* of playing with words, playing with language, playing with image, in fact playing with the real building bricks of poetry. It records that experience in the only way our youngest children can, which is by drawing.

And yet look at it! Can this seriously be called a poem? It hardly seems like the sort of thing one is likely to find in a children's anthology – *The Oxford First Poetry Book* series, for example, – or even in the 'whackier' works of writers such as Colin McNaughton. When can one call a piece of writing a poem and when not? Are there different categories for what constitutes children's poetry and adult poetry and if so, what are they? These are the legitimate worries of the uncertain teacher/writer. These are what constitute the poem's 'wobble'. These are the stumbling blocks out of which this construction was built. These are the questions on which this poem, its writer and teacher, might come a cropper. Perhaps, indeed, that is the risk one takes if one plays around in the writing process. However, in the case of this poem, it is a risk which pays off because, paradoxically, where this poem 'falls down' is where it succeeds.

The poem, I think, succeeds because its presiding image – the building of construction blocks – functions as an effective image holding in playful tension three different events. It overlays the child's unsteady hand playing with building bricks with the teacher's uncertain handling of poem-building while, at the same time, underlaying both of these with the image of words as building blocks and the whole process of the poem as a play on building itself. Its authenticity as a poem lies in the unsteady, uncertain hands involved in a wobbly process anticipating a final, delightful collapse.

PAINTING

paintbrush tickles page
until hole giggles
its way through painting
wetting itself with
the laughing

This second poem is the result of the teacher's observation of her Junior Infant's first painting session of the year. The merging of product and process – the actual painting and the act of painting – is reflected in the poem's blurred grammatical unpunctuated form. These blurred edges hint at the fusion of the painter and the painting. At no stage is a definite product, a picture, mentioned; the word 'painting' functions as both noun and verb. It fuses doing-the-naming, and naming-the-doing. Just as a water colour blends colours, in this poem the various elements of the experience – the brush, the page, the laughter, the hole – are water-coloured together in a fluid unity. The poem's form appears like the image on a photograph out of its developing solution, as Creation appears out of a misty Genesis. Indeed, the activity of painting might well function as a developing fluid for the personality of the child.

The community within which the child lives also functions as a 'developing fluid':

> Would you live in Stabannon if you had the choice?
> There's the school there's the pub
> There's the church and the youth club
> And then there's Richard
> Stabannon's main man
> Who'll hold his head high
> Just to show that he can.
> Would you live in Stabannon
> if you had the choice?

Brid, 5th Class

On first reading, Brid's poem about her locality seems rather weightless, lame, a poem which never really got going. It had arisen out of a unit of local history involving an exploration of the monuments, gravestones, placenames, townlands of the locality, together with a rough census of the area. On closer reading, however, Brid's opening question hinted at a struggle to commit herself, to believe in her local community being worth writing about. At the sub-textual level, it points to a struggle to commit her energy to the task, almost a 'would you – that is, the audience, that is the teacher – write this poem if you had the choice?' There is a very important question in these opening lines about the nature of power relations in the class-room and the role of Art (poetry in this particular instance) in the midst of those power relations. But perhaps the best way to explore that question is to stick closely to the poem itself. Brid's doubt about her local community having anything to recommend itself or mark its significance may have echoed the community's shallow faith in itself as anything special. Her doubt may also reflect Brid's own shal-low faith in her ability to write a poem which would turn out to be anything special. After all, in a national context, this area of the country was best known in a radio and TV advertisement spoken by a flat-accented, wellied, peak-capped farmer, as being 'only an hour from Dublin'. Only its relative distance from the country's capital gave Brid's locality any significance, analogous perhaps, to the fact that the only significance many adults give to children's poetry is its relative closeness to adult poetry, not for any inherent value it might have in expressing an accurate view of children's reality. The com-munity's diffidence may have been an echo of some rather negative national feeling, expressed in collective self-accusations that the coun-try's politicians were going cap-in-hand to the European Community to look for all the structural funding they could get for this tiny country existing on Europe's periphery. Of course, it would be absurd to suggest that these latter levels of significance existed in the conscious mind of the writer as she wrote her poem, but they are testimony to the nature of one of the 'gifts' of poetry rather than its deliberate 'craft' in this particular instance, that, in the process of making a poem, it may acquire resonances and meanings not initially part of the in-tention of the writer at all, a gift which Heaney compared to that of the water diviner or the dowser – something which could not be learned or acquired:

. . . a gift for being in touch with what is there, hidden and real, a gift for mediating between the latent resource and the community that wants it current and released.[6]

It would be the responsibility of the teacher as 'close-reader' to explain this gift to the pupil and, paraphrasing Patrick Kavanagh, to

nourish in her the idea that 'poetry must be allowed to surprise us'.
In the discovery of 'the extra-ordinary in the ordinary', the poem
begins to grow in significance, both at the level of task and at the level
of meaning of the poem itself. This is a lot of what the writer was
struggling with in her first draft. In this way the teacher can help the
poem to 'quicken' in its writer and to become, as Professor Cox puts
it, 'vigorous, committed, honest and interesting'.[7] 'There's the school
there's the pub/There's the church and the youth club' suggest a
bored eleven-year old giving a perfunctory polite tour of the locality
to a visitor whose interest in the place seems unwarranted. The temp-
tation of an 'arm's-length' reading of this poem would be to collude
with the mood of the writer and move on to some other place, some
other poem, more interesting, more promising. In essence, the teacher/
tourist has asked for a conducted tour of this child's locality and,
within the power relations of the classroom, that request is being
complied with. The poem seeks to comply with the teacher's 'powerful invitation' to write and at the same time to say as little as possible.
But however little is being said, much more is being meant.

The writer in this case has offered a tour of the institutional locality. The church, the pub, the school and the youth club are the corner
stones of every ordinary rural parish. Their ordinariness goes hand-
in-hand with their being fundamental to it and vice-versa. Description
of them has no need to be elaborate. It is sufficient for the writer
simply to state the fact of their being. The rhyming of 'pub' and 'club'
establishes a pairing between these two over and against the other
two, the school and the church, which then, by implication, also
form a pair. (Indeed, physically they look straight at each other from
opposite sides of the road.) The implications of the tensions inherent in their hidden relationships, – as opposed to a 'nothing to hide,
– it's out there in rhyme and sound' – constitute a source of on-going
controversy in the history of the State. Again, these are levels of significance which have not been consciously willed by the writer, but
nevertheless they are there and to point to them is to affirm poetry-
as-gift, in the actual experience of the writer.

Life in this poem is seen in the context of the institutions within
which it is lived, as opposed to the physical environment – nature

and rural setting. The perception of this eleven-year old, expressed via the poem, hints at a dawning consciousness of an understanding of the social world. This understanding has cast the poem in a territory of meaning between the two worlds which constitute it – the institution and the individual:

> And then there's Richard
> Stabannon's main man
> Who'll hold his head high
> Just to show that he can.

The writer's presentation of Richard is immediately energetic, rhythmic, rhyming, confident and definite. It contrasts not only the individual with the institution, but interest with boredom, energy with apathy, individual identity with institutional anonymity. Richard is a self-declaration of individual freedom, (an interesting symbol in this poem, given the suspicions about the power-relations of the classroom), as against collective dependence. Perhaps it is Richard, perhaps it is the individual, perhaps it is freedom, perhaps it is just 'being oneself' which need no justification or explanation other than childhood's direct answer to every 'why?' – 'Just!' Richard stands four-square over and against the basic institutions of rural living, head and shoulders above the rest of the community, a position underlined by the phrase 'Stabannon's main man'. Richard is obvious; Richard is a 'show'; Richard is a challenge to the collective hidden agenda implicit in the first part of the poem.

The poem, in its energy, its mood, its pattern, seems cyclical; it ends as it began, with the question:

> Would you live in Stabannon
> if you had the choice?

But the question with which the writer began , despite its appearance, is not exactly the same as the one she ends with, because the actual writing of the poem has altered it. Indeed, the reading of the poem has also deepened the close reader's understanding of the locality. It is as though in her repetition, the writer holds the question of the creative tension between the individual and the institution in society – a much more creative act than simply giving one or other of them the 'last word' – in the last line. The repetition of 'you' in the final question springs the poem, like a trap, back on to its readers, challenging each to decide one way or another, to choose which Stabannon to live in. The trick in the challenge is hidden in the last line,' if you had the choice'. Children as a sub-cultural group have little or no choice about where they live; adults assume that they, as adults, do have choice. The arms-length reader will read the last lines –

> Would you live in Stabannon
> if you had the choice?

as one, seduced into doing so by the absence of a capital 'i' on 'if'. To read the last two lines as one particularises choice in relation to the proper definite noun, Stabannon. The sting in the tail of these sub-cultural linguistics lies in what is known as a 'diachronic' and 'synchronic' overlap in the word 'choice'. Its relatedness to the question is not only diachronic, that is, its meaning is gained from its position in relation to other words and their position in the sentence – in this instance, it relates particularly to Stabannon – but synchronically, it plumbs the depths of the word 'choice' itself: that is, 'choice', meaning the act of choosing, the power or right to choose as well as 'choice' meaning worthy of being chosen, selected, or of special excellence. The question of choice in its relation to what and whom are central to the poem, as indeed they are to life itself. In this way the poem is a kind of metaphor for the power-struggle between childhood and adulthood, between authority and dependence, between individuality and collectivity, between dominant culture and sub-culture.

This is the reluctant writer's first draft of the poem. Building a first sense of 'crafting' into a more substantial skill is part of the drafting process. Through it the writer learns to refine a poem from its first spontaneous but blurred form – a steadying of the hand so that the bricks don't wobble. Drafting is a process which must allow time, since often time itself brings change. It may not be appropriate to attempt to redraft a poem during the same lesson in which it was written, since language, like paint or clay, may need time to set before further work can be done on it.

The second draft of this poem tried to 'heavy-outline' Richard against the background of where he lives, by highlighting detail, by colouring him in a bit:

> Would you live in Stabannon
> if you had the choice?
>
> There's the school for the children
> There's the pub for the men
> There's the church for the women
> There's the youth club for in-between.
> Richard doesn't fit anywhere there
> He just walks the roads, he doesn't care.
> Richard is Stabannon's main man
> Who'll hold his head high
> Just to show that he can.
> He'll smoke in your face
> Flick his ash with such grace
> Smile all down the aisle from Communion
>
> Would you live in Stabannon
> if you had the choice?

Draft two is significantly more detailed. Institutional images have been coloured in with their membership, but are still general, non-personalised. Taken singly, we have no more knowledge of them than we had initially; taken collectively, we see further into their gendered and generational 'segregated interdependence', most immediately represented in the mixed-up world of the 'in-between' youth. The image of Richard has been highlighted. He has been further coloured in with rhyme and movement and action and smiles. One senses in the broad-vowelled rhyming of 'aisle' and 'smile', an immense ear-to-ear grin. It is a smile which is too broad to be devious, yet wide enough to let us see the twinkle in the 'ai', perhaps reflecting a lightness in the head – or a lightness in the soul.   Richard is the seemingly 'simple', yet sub-consciously very complex archetypal character, who lives in the soul of the rural Irish community.   He has within him something of 'The Bird' in John B. Keane's *The Field* and Patrick Kavanagh's 'Green Fool'. The challenge of his 'smoke-in-your-face', allied with the graceful flick of politically incorrect cigarette ash, hints at a connoisseurship, an ability to breathe deeply one's delicate mortality and puff it skywards, almost in the community's face: to spit in life's eye. The full significance of 'Communion' may not be within the poet's intellectual grasp, but the keenness of her observations suggest that she knows Richard very well and balances him delicately, smiling and challenging his and her own background.

The consultation process between teacher and writer resulted in the discarding of 'Richard doesn't fit . . . he doesn't care', since they seemed to speak *for* Richard instead of letting Richard speak for himself. They robbed the poem, by over-explaining, of some of its tension. It was also decided that the third draft might make more use of the proper noun 'Richard', in order to sharpen contrast and further emphasise individuality. It was also to be hoped that this repetition might almost become a 'nuisance', and thereby make another comment on the individual concerned, though such a hope would only be vindicated or negated in speaking the poem. In any case, it had to be tried in order to see if it worked:

> Would you live in Stabannon
> if you had the choice?
>
> There's the school for the children
> There's the pub for the men,
> There's the church for the women,
> There's the youth-club for in-between.
> And then there's Richard,
> Stabannon's main man.
> Richard holds his head high,
> Just to show that Richard can,

Richard smokes in your face,
Flicks his ash with such grace,
Richard smiles down the aisle from Communion.

Would you live in Stabannon
if you had the choice?

We decided that this draft worked well and only needed a title to finish it off. Finding a title for a poem is not always easy and the learning inherent in naming one's poem should not be underestimated. In naming her poem the writer comes to a total sense of the poem as a finished work, echoing what Heaney says about 'Right' naming as 'the first foundation/For telling truth'.[8] In this case, the writer – perhaps caught in the middle of those tensions she manages so successfully in the poem – hesitates between the titles 'Richard', 'Stabannon' and 'Choices'. The teacher suggested 'Communion' since it seemed capable of holding nuances of all three, but later withdrew the suggestion as inappropriate adult sophistication or just smartness. Ironically, the title eventually arrived at was 'You Choose', which, of course, suits the poem perfectly.

Just as the title of a poem is important, so also is the act of signing one's name to the poem one has made. The stamp of this personal hallmark is important in developing the writer's psychological sense of him/herself as a writer. Such a sense may be well rounded in the mature writer but in the 'shy soul' it must be nourished and affirmed, both in the writing and speaking of the poem. To identify oneself with one's poems in the signing of one's name is continually to identify oneself as a poet, with a growing sense of the truth in that naming too.

READY STEADY – NO

Can you jump into a poem
Like you jump into a pool
Or do you sit on the edge
And dabble your words
A toe or two at a time?

Catriona, 3rd Class

TRYING IT ON

One day I made myself a poem.
I tried it on.
I looked in the mirra.
The buttons were done up
Wrong.

Grace, 2nd Class

POEM MAKING

I soloed
I dodged
I aimed
I kicked
I watched,
breathless
...WIDE!

Darragh, 4th Class

POEM SWITCH

I grope for a poem switch
In my head
But it's all dark in there
I can't find the light
To write.

Grace, 6th Class

STICKY POETRY

It's stuck to my jumper like fluff;
Poetry is strange sorta stuff;
It's stuck like a tat in my hair -
However it got tangled up there,
It's stuck to my fingers like jam,
And I'm licking it still, so I am,

And it's stuck like a fly in my eye,
And it's making it water and cry;
It's stuck on my knee like the grime
Of the plaster's left-over black line,
It's stuck on my tongue like a hair,
That came from -
I don't know where,

So where does poetry come from?
                              5th, 6th Class

All of these poems are a conscious savouring of the process of writing as well as the delight in words themselves; they celebrate the craft of making, as well as the gift of being able to say something about the act of doing it – in particular, the problems and pains associated with it. This type of poem is particularly useful to the nervous or uncertain teacher, precisely because of its dual functioning. In the process of the writing lies the learning – the business of education and the educator – hence, in this type of poem, the learner/writer and the learner/teacher meet.

The consciousness of the experience of trying to make or write a poem is, of course, central to the life of the poet. Many poets have written about the business of writing. For example, Heaney in *Preoccupations* recalls one of his early attempts at writing, when he signs himself '*Incertus*' – 'uncertain, a shy soul fretting and all that.'[9] This underlying emotional uncertainty (as prevalent in the teacher as in the pupil) is echoed in 'Ready Steady – No', in which the hesitancy about jumping into the pool acts as a metaphor for the emotion of uncertainty in the act of writing. It is an experience of being poised on the edge and trying, as Heaney suggests, to 'Make impulse one with wilfulness, and enter'[10] the poem's current, its 'steady purchase and thrum.'[11] 'Poem Making' echoes the processes identified with the football image in Heaney's poem, 'The Point',[12] with its effort to 'score' a poem:

Was it you

or the ball that kept going
beyond you . . .

– or, indeed, was it the poem itself? The student-poet's experience of failure resonates with Heaney's

. . . fabulous high-catcher
coming down without the ball[13]

In 'Trying It On', one suspects the presence of fingers – perhaps
numinous – like Heaney's 'little antic fish' which 'are all go', 'Down
between the lines' of the poem, which the poet 'sees' in the meaning
of '*Claritas*'.[14] In all of these poems there is a process, a pattern of
work which is capable of giving as much satisfaction to the writer as
the craft of Heaney's farmer in 'Man and Boy' who

. . . has mown himself to the centre of the field
And stands in a final perfect ring
Of sunlit stubble. [15]

The child, with the guidance of the teacher, has written his or her
experience of the writing process into the centre of the poem's image.
Consequently, even though the emotion to be correlated is one of
failure, because the process is authentic in the accuracy of the image
chosen to represent that emotion, the poems succeed; they exemplify
what Heaney calls 'a congruence between impulse and right action';[16]
they are almost suggestive of a poetry which writes itself.

Overlapping the act of writing with the thinking about writing
typifies much of what has already been said about children's reality.
Much of the poetry which will generate and be generated by this kind
of reality is essentially a poetic praxis: in essence, it fuses the theory
and the practice of poetry writing into the single act. At certain
points in this process, the teacher may speak about methodology; for
example, in 'Poem Switch', the method being practised was to take

an emotion – a mixture of frustration and 'lostness' – and find an image for it:

It's like when you're in bed and you waken because you have to go to the toilet and it's dark and you don't know where you are and you're trying to find the light switch and you know it's there but still, you can't find it and you have to grope around . . . .

Then let that experience stand for what it's like to be trying to find an idea for a poem and mix the two things together. Instead of a light switch, make it a poem switch; instead of trying to see, you are trying to write; the darkness is not in your room but inside your head. This kind of approach can be practised, but the real 'happening' of poetry will be a fusion in word of thought and act. The central resource in this kind of process is the language which precedes 'thought', the image, which Gertrude Patterson has examined closely in relation to the work of the Imagists and the method of composition adopted by T. S. Eliot. She quotes the French critic, Rémy de Gourmont and T. E. Hulme in support of her thesis. De Gourmont stated that 'On pense au moyen d'images',[17] or as T. E. Hulme put it:

Thought is prior to language and consists in the simultaneous presentation to the mind of two different images. Language is only a more or less feeble way of doing this.[18]

In its potency, image is, in a sense, the way, the truth and the life of poetry. The more potent the image, the more generative it is of new metaphor and symbol, the fuller will be its poetic life.

Enabling and encouraging pupils to search for and learn how to manipulate the image is the approach to writing advocated and described by Patterson in the previous chapters. She suggests that it is the responsiblity of the teacher as writer to discover where and how to look and hence to teach young writers something of the same process. It is not an easy task, given the conceptual, analytical urges of our scientific, functional and 'plain-speaking' culture. The process of looking for image which can then serve for what Eliot defined as the 'formula' or 'objective correlative'[19] for an emotion, implies that, when it is found, there is in it something hidden – a hidden meaning, a hidden reality or hidden agenda. The hidden is what allows the image to be fresh, to surprise, to evoke in the reader that spontaneous 'Ah! Yes!' in the discovery of the experience which it evokes. The obvious is what renders most speech plain and therefore, as Hulme argued, imprecise and ineffective. Such a search is parallelled in a class group-search of the 'hide-outs' in their own houses for 'Lost and Found':

LOST AND FOUND

Even if they're found
They'll soon be lost again

– the keys of the car
– the baby's bottle
– Mammy's purse
– the remote control
– the scissors and sellotape

And found
– down the back of the sofa
– under the telly
– out in the car
– fallen into the coal bucket
– in the jam-jar behind the curtain on the kitchen
                                                window
– in the bottom of my schoolbag

– where I left it.

                              3rd,4th Class

In the process of searching for precise image lies the learning opportunity for refining the crude image into sheer image. Sheerness lies in the image's freshness and accuracy. In order to find out whether or not an image is fresh, children must test it out by squeezing it like a loaf on the shelf of the corner shop. They must learn to ask questions of it in order to sort out stale images from fresh ones. In the midst of generalised images they must learn to ask specific questions so that the image is particularised, pin-pointed in their own individual experience. The first images children offer for an emotion or an event, for example, are often couched in abstract propositions:

> Boring is when you're fed up.
> Boring is when you've nothing to do.
> Boring is when you've no one to play with.

But here are more specific, more sharply pin-pointed images of boredom:

> Boring is the tin of biscuits when the fancy ones are all eaten
> Boring is when the ball won't bounce
> Boring is Sunday afternoon when the grown-ups sleep
> with the papers
> Boring is when the fizz is all out of the Coke
> Boring is Daniel O'Donnell on Top of the Pops.

Just as the previous chapter shows that metaphor needs to be based on the literal world of observation, children find it easier to identify fresh images if they are wrapped in a personally-experienced actuality. Take, for example, these images of spring:

SPRING IS

> – Taking off your shoes and socks to race in the grass
> – Smelling the newly cut lawn
> – Tying your jumper around your waist
> – White legs and arms
> – Not many swans left on the bog
> – The feeling to go for a walk

– First time you take your bike instead of the school bus
– Salad instead of hot dinner
– Not noticing that the fire's out.

3rd, 4th Class

as opposed to

SPRING IS

– snowdrops and daffodils
– animals come out of hibernation
– leaves come on the trees
– the birds sing
– the lambs play in the fields

In the first poem, the language is exact because it is directly linked to the experiences of the class and their ability to 'observe' them accurately in the images which convey them. In the second, on the other hand, the images may, of course, be real, but are more likely to be the received images in which spring is stereotyped.

Images may often hide in the most ordinary looking words and, just as it is pointless to send a child off to look for something precise in a vague place with vague directions, children, especially those whose linguistic sensitivity has been dulled by their environment, succeed best when they are given constructive help. It can be useful to turn words 'upside-down' or 'shake' them and see what falls out, or stretch and poke them. 'Technic-ly Speaking' was the result of one child's rummage through one of his favourite books – the Argos catalogue. Taking all the technical modern sounding words he could find, he built the following:

TECHNIC-LY SPEAKING

Answering machine
Opened the door

C.D. said 'Hi! Fi!'
Fax relaxed with some micro-chips
So Micro waved 'bye-bye'.
She decided to go for a Walkman
Although she didn't N-intend to
Then she Fast-Tracked back
For a Mega Drive
Around to the Kar-y-out.
OK then?

Mark, 5th Class

This is a technically constructed poem built with Lego-type words. One senses in its robotic composure and metallic colour the enjoyment of a poetry mechanic with bits and pieces of words scattered around his workbench. Mechanically speaking, it is poetry and a legitimate enterprise for its author. One is reminded of Miroslav Holub, quoted by Heaney, when he says:

I like writing for people untouched by poetry; for instance, for those who do not even know that it should be at all for them. I would like them to read poems as naturally as they read the papers, or go to a football game.[20]

Much is made of the view that poetry for children should be fun – and so it should. Child's play is seriously enjoyable for the participants and so also should it be with the child's play with words. The following is an example of poems which are serious play:

SUM MASTER!

Sum how
Sumtime
Sumwhere
Sumone or

Sumthing
Will tell the master to
Sum-up
(But not me!)

                                        3rd, 4th Class

POOR ME

Poor me
Poor me
It's always the same
I wanted it fancy
It ended up plain.

Poor me
Poor me
It's terribly sad
For when I'm without it
It drives me quite mad!

                                        Brid, 5th Class

THE ARGOS CATALOGUE

Imagine an Argos catalogue
Of 'Poems and Rhymes'
All for something pounds
Ninety-nine!
(a poetic bargain)

                                        Ciara, 6th Class

As well as being fun, these word-plays are what Heaney calls his 'first
sense of crafting words'.[21]

The relationship of poetry to the social, historical and cultural
context in which it expresses itself – the relationship of Art to Life – is
a tense one. Concerned, like Heaney, that the sociopolitical testimony be at least offered to children at that stage when they begin to

concern themselves with issues in today's world, the teacher must attempt to nourish poetic consciousness and conscience. However, the development of the child-poet's voice is open to abuse by the personal whim of the teacher who has not weighed herself, as Heaney says, 'hand and foot, in the scale of things.'[22] Hence, the teacher must strive for a balanced approach to the relationship between 'Song and Suffering'.

The occasion of a visit to the Dail to meet the Minister for Overseas Development and be congratulated for raising funds for the Third World, seemed an appropriate opportunity to explore the relationship between poetry and reality, in this case, the Third World. The poem below is the class result of that exploration. This poem was inscribed on a hand-made feeding bowl which was presented to the Minister:

GRAMMAR OF LIFE

I am hungry
You are hungry
He is hungry
She is hungry
We are hungry
You are hungry
They are hungry

5th, 6th Class

As a poem, it is a statement made in a political context, of the way things are at the core, basic level of the verb 'to be'. It is a verb declined and defined by hunger. It is a hunger to be: a hunger to live. But again, as Heaney says, 'Hearing and value do not always entail a lofty note and an earnest message'.[23]

LIVING ROOM

I was watching the telly
And on came the news

I saw these black children,
No food, no clothes, no shoes.
I thought, 'This is awful
I'll put a stop to that.'
I went in to the telly
Made a friend,
Had a chat.

'Come on out here
To my living room with me
You can share some of my clothes
And I'll give you your tea.
I'm sure my jeans would fit you
And my other runners – size two,
And sausage, beans and chips for tea
Will that be O.K. for you?'

'What's your name?
Where do you live?
Where do you go to school?
Who's your best friend?
When is your birthday ?
Would you like to go to the pool?
Do you like Michael Jackson?
Did you see 'Home Alone'?
What age are your brothers and sisters?
Have you also got a bike of your own?
Isn't it better living here?
Sure stay . . . Why not? . . . For Good!'

But she only said in a whispery voice
'I want to go home'.

3rd, 4th Class

It is not surprising that the form arrived at in much of our group writing had the strong pattern and rhyme associated with the ballad. One senses that there may be three possible reasons for this. Having abandoned the relative safety and privacy of individual writing, the strong rhythmic form and pattern of the ballad acts as a safety net in the face of group chaos. Also, the form itself may lie just below the surface of our cultural psyche, like the songlines of the Australian aborigines, like psycho-cultural lines of longitude and latitude, a kind of invisible under-net. Thirdly, narrative is the normal vehicle of children's thoughts; storying is for them a primary act of consciousness, not only individually but collectively as well. The group narrative poem has not only an important place in the writing process, but also in the saying process, that is, in the making of 'sound-sense' for the child. The ballad form and its recitation are inseparable. Recitation, according to the *Oxford English Dictionary*, is 'a musical declamation, intermediate between singing and ordinary speech'. This narrative mediation between ordinary speech and song is exemplified in the ballad form, an intrinsic part of the literary tradition of these islands. Its mediatory role is particularly useful in exploring poetry because it provides a bridge for the story between prose and free verse – a bridge for the voice between spoken and sung, between oral and written.

In the past, the ballad form has provided a sociological bridge between those whose tradition has been oral, that is, a non-literate working class, and those of a literate upper class. It has also the vocal resonance which, as Heaney put it, 'gave verse, however humble, a place in the life of the home, made it one of the ordinary rituals of life.'[24] It has done much the same for the life of the school. Its rhythm and formal pattern are sturdy blocks for working with, composed, as the Imagist F. S. Flint or Ezra Pound defined it in another context 'in sequence of a metronome.'[25] In its distance from the rhythms of everyday speech, therefore, it often reflects more of a cartoon-type reality than complex human reality. It is a kind of poetic-puppetry, but a legitimate art-form nonetheless in introducing pupils to the made-world of the poem.

THE PUPPET MAN

The puppet man with his puppet clan
Came to our school to-day.
He said, 'Well! Hello! Will you come to my show?'
He said 'Ready ! Steady! 'Let's go!'

A wig and a hat, a joke and a chat,
A song and a clap and a bow;
There was laughter and after the water got squirted,
We giggled and sniggled, 'What now?'

Said Mark, 'What the heck 'bout a sword in the neck,
It's only a trick, so I'll try it!'
His laugh sounded hollow as he tried not to swallow,
Now all of a sudden he's quiet!

Behind the striped canvas, the puppets lay handless,
Awaiting their turn to impress us,
Which they did more and more and we shouted 'Encore!'
But he's gone with his puppets. God bless us!

(And them too.)

5th, 6th Class

Any action which a human being undertakes requires energy.
There are different kinds of energy, but within the classroom, the
energy required to write poetry is of a very particular kind. It is very
different from the type of energy required to sustain the normal run-
of-the-school-day, which is even-keeled, what Heaney called a 'steady
purchase and thrum' kind of energy. Sometimes, as a class teacher,
one can sit back momentarily and hear the steady drone of this energy humming through the classroom.   But this hum-drum-drone
kind of energy is, I suspect, anaesthetising over the course of a day, a
week, a term, a year and indeed, over the course of a lifetime. The
more this kind of energy predominates in poetry classes, the less likely
it is that any real poetry will be written in school. Consequently, it is

often the case that the kind of energy required to write poetry is an initial high-booster, or a strong depth-charge, a kick-start kind of energy to wrench oneself and one's class out of the predominant quasi-comatose state. This, I feel, is particularly true of the more senior classes whose day tends to have more routine and less physical activity than the infant classes. But how can one access this kind of energy? The truth is that it is not always possible, even with the best will in the world, to tap into 'poetic energy'. It takes an experienced and sensitive teacher to recognise a chink in the armour of the routine and to grab hold of it urgently as though it were a devious leprechaun. This kind of 'chink-in-the-day's-armour' is both an opportunity and a crisis which, as Ted Hughes suggests,

. . . rouses the brain's resources: the compulsion towards haste overthrows the ordinary precautions, flings everything into top gear, and many things that are usually hidden find themselves rushed in to the open. Barriers break down, prisoners come out of their cells.[26]

When literature concerning a poetry competition lands on the teacher's desk, it may be unwelcome,,,given the over-emphasis on competition in education already, or it may present one of those moments of motivational crisis/opportunity. The latter was the case in terms of Ruth's poem:

HIDEOUT

I live beside a
Field of ideas.

I made a poem hut there
Out of words and branches and twigs.

There are cows wondering
In my field of ideas.

Cows knock
My poem hut down.

They think my field of ideas
Is theirs to eat.

Cows don't understand my poetry.

Ruth, 4th Class[27]

Ruth's poem is a straightforward enough overlapping of two ideas –
the idea of building a poem and the idea of building a hut. The words
and images taken from the child's actual experience of building a hut
out of branches and things is super-imposed on the experience of
writing a poem, which is more difficult to articulate. Working with a
poem in this way is like working with one of those little mosaic-type
puzzles in which one slides the various squares over and back and up
and down, to try to arrive at the completed picture, or the numbers
in the correct sequence. The writer has to arrive, after a process of
drafting and redrafting, at a decision about which words, from the
two basic images, belong where. In this way, words such as 'ideas',
'words', 'poem' are implanted in the physical landscape of the poem,
among words such as 'fields', 'branches', 'huts', 'cows' and so on.

In the midst of this process, Ruth's poem 'happened' upon a little
gem of a linguistic coincidence which I feel pays homage to a poem's
capacity to surprise even its author. Ruth is a very polite little girl
who makes every effort to speak with an 'elocuted' voice. I believe
that, as Ruth concentrated on writing the final draft 'in her very best
handwriting', she was also saying the poem into herself 'in her very
best speaking voice'. The overlap of voice and hand resulted in a little
linguistic 'tweak' and she wrote 'wondering' instead of 'wandering'.
When I, as teacher, read this, I was very excited. This was no longer
'a straightforward enough' poem, owing more to hard graft/craft than
anything else. The poem, of its own accord almost, had quickened.
The freak 'tweak' had transformed those cows from dumb wandering animals, into beings with the power to 'wonder': to 'wonder'
about poetry! How absolutely wonderful! One could see their fabulous, huge, round eyes, like capital 'O's, fill with amazement as they
'wandered' and 'wondered' through that field of ideas. That transfor-

mation from 'a' to 'o', was pivotal; it became the axis around which
the poem turned and was turned into a living, breathing, moving
entity. And yet it is only one letter away from 'wandering'; one cannot 'wonder' in a hurry; wandering is the natural pace at which one
wonders and the natural pace at which cows move. But perhaps the
best – or at least, the most significant, was yet to come. Perhaps Ruth's
last line – 'Cows don't understand my poetry', was singularly pro-
phetic, because, when her poem was published as one of the winning
entries for the Telepoem competition, that 'o' had been 'corrected'
and those wonderfilled cows had been reduced to their lower order:
to their dumb 'wanderings'. Ruth and I know, however, that it isn't
those cows in the fields that didn't understand her poem!

INCISION

Massive Ferguson
unzips the chest of the hill;
gulls like white corpuscles
spill into the sky.

This poem was written by the teacher in the role ascribed to her
by the Cox Report, that of modelling the success the pupils should
strive for.[28] It is a poem which presents various particulars – ploughing, tractor, hill, unzipping, chest, gulls' flight and so on – in what
Wheelwright refers to as 'diverse particulars in a newly designed arrangement'.[29] Its usefulness as an example of the writing process lies
in the example it offers of the making of an image by creating new
metaphor. The meaning of 'ploughing' is extended by comparing it
to an 'unzipping'; juxtaposing this unzipping with 'the chest of the
hill' combines the two into new meaning. By a similar metaphoric
process in the last two lines, gulls – a relatively common and concrete
'vehicular image' – are identified with white corpuscles, less well known
as an observable part of the everyday world of reality. The poem then
goes on to create new meaning by arranging or synthesising the white
corpuscles and gulls with 'spill into the sky'. This arrangement is
facilitated by already-existing associations of spilling, with blood, but

immediately dislocates any presuppositions by reversing the direction of that spill – towards the sky rather than towards the earth. Taken together, these two metaphors constitute a single 'œuvre': the unzipping and the spilling are one, linked and joined in the poem's presiding image of ploughing. For children who live close to, and in many cases make their living directly off the land, the central metaphor of the poem – ploughing – is a routine, common-sense, unemotional operation. Its clinical nature is reflected in the poem's curt-cut title 'Incision', a purposeful and carefully calculated opening-up, as opposed to a rough careless gash. What is being expressed is the nature of this routine 'agri-surgical' operation. The poem simply presents an image and leaves it at that: the reader must take it or leave it. The underlying emotion of the poem is the serious and emotionally disciplined relationship between farming and its environment. It depersonalises the relationship of the writer from what is being written about.

At another level this poem describes a symbolic wound – a common symbol for poetry itself. The wound in this case is not a deep one, which may suggest that the writer has not yet developed the poetic capacity or skills to dig deep into poetry's underground. Or its shallowness may be in respect of the childhood context in which the poem was written; the topsoil may be childhood's legitimate terrain. One senses however that those white corpuscles spilling into the heavens may be symbolic of the fruits of massive effort on the part of the writer. Certainly the 'massive' in the opening line is very much out of proportion with the ease of effort in 'unzipping' and 'spilling'. If, as Heaney says, poetry is a 'poetry revelation of the self to the self',[30] then this poem may reveal to the writer something in herself of the relationship of poetry's gifts and the 'effort to write'. Bearing in mind also Heaney's remarks about 'poetry as a dig, a dig for finds that end up being plants',[31] this poem will confirm for its writer and for those she teaches, that, despite the ease with which it was written, in poetry there is indeed a lot more digging than finding!

The following poem is a further example of the teacher as writer, this time exploring the relationship between words and the reality they represent:

LY-CRO LANGUAGE

Lycra language stretches
To fit precisely
What a body needs to say.
No sagging of the bottom
Line, no bagging at the knees,
Or droopy jowled vowels, tongue-in-cheek.
It has plenty of give
To let the voice breathe
In and out without fear
Or falling apart at the seams.

Velcro-speak fastens meaning in place
For as long as needs be
Bound to society.
But snitched asunder
What words have joined together;
Lips part, and the mouth is free
To shout it
Or shut it – quietly.

Reality is obviously not 'fixed'. The reality of the world we live in is the reality of on-going change. In order to capture this changing reality, language itself needs to be flexible. It needs to have an elasticity which allows it to move with the times. It needs to have the capacity to hold fast to the changing nature of things and ideas. 'Lycra language' and 'Velcro speak' are tongue-in-cheek-images which attempt to explore the situation in which language attempts to fasten and fashion itself to fit the new, the constantly-changing. It is a modern 'fabrication' of the truth of that situation. They are synthetic images rather than the natural-fibred poem which 'Incision' is. But they are an authentic attempt to realise poetic language's inherent capacity to offer people – and in this instance – the children in our classrooms, the material they need to hold down their world by learning how to define it accurately. In the unstable, erratic, yet exciting world in which they live, to be engaged in the writing proc-

esses of poetry is to be engaged in developing language skills which
can help equip the child to control, to manage and hence to order
the on-going chaos of living in today's world – and finally, perhaps,
to live in it, sustained by the meanings they have made from it.

Reading back over these pages, I am aware of the extent to which
I have referred to the work of Seamus Heaney and wonder, why
Heaney? Is it, perhaps, because we share a common background in
Heaney's 'country of community',[32] the 'wells and dunghills'[33] of
Annahorish? 'The lough waters/Can petrify wood',[34] and petrified
me too, on many a Sunday afternoon as I sat in my father's small boat
and thought – 'so much water, so little me'. Perhaps it was this country of community – Ballymaguigan, Castledawson and the Toome
Road along which I travelled to school each day – which fostered
'bedding the ear' with the 'linguistic hard-core'[35] out of which to speak
and hear Heaney's poetry. Equally importantly, however, it may also
have rescued the notion of 'the poet' from being associated in my
mind only with 'foreigners', who, I gathered as a schoolgirl, lived
either in England or in the past. Heaney, on the other hand, as Patrick
Kavanagh puts it, enthroned the poet at home, 'king/Of banks and
stones and every blooming thing.'[36] The poet was no longer foreign.

Or is it the teacher in Heaney and the advice he gives to the beginning poet?

And your first steps as a writer will be to imitate, consciously or uncon-
sciously, those sounds that flowed in, that in-fluence.[37]

or

Yet in practice, you proceed by your own experience of what it is to
write what you consider a successful poem. You survive in your own
esteem not by the corroboration of theory but by the trust in certain
moments of satisfaction which you know intuitively to the moments of
extension.[38]

Or perhaps it had more to do with the rather shocking sight of
what, at one point, I considered a 'throughother' handwritten manuscript copy of the poem 'North' which we studied as part of the poetry

course I referred to earlier. With its scribbles and crossings-out and a rather 'uncomposed' appearance, it seemed a far cry from 'another accomplished print-out'[39] of the form in which I had encountered poems up until then. Seeing this manuscript, I recalled a musician friend who used to go and watch his favourite band as they rehearsed, prior to a concert. In doing so, he could see them make and correct mistakes, practise certain phrases over and over again and, as they did so, reveal the intricate skills involved in playing an instrument. This process he always found much more entertaining than the polished performance.

Perhaps it was then the pedagogic insights offered with the authority and authenticity of a 'real' practising writer which were particularly valuable to someone whose function as a teacher herself, and then as a student embarked on a poetry course, required that she should not only learn how to write poetry herself but teach her pupils how to write as well.

These are some of the conscious reasons why I have been so strongly influenced by my course of study on poetry writing and Heaney's work. But not everything that influences one is of a conscious or rational nature. Heaney's influence on me, in its deeper dimensions, has, I suspect, been quite non-rational. Initially, indeed, and perhaps surprisingly, it was not Heaney's poetry that made an impression on me. Like most pupils at school of my generation and since, I had been 'taught' 'Mid-Term Break'. Poems at that stage of my career belonged to one of two categories: hard poems or easy poems. This one was easy, that is, you could tell what it was about. It stated the case in straight lines and left it at that. But the teaching of it didn't leave it at that. Neither did my suspicions. Even at that age, my trust in contrariness was well developed, although it has to be said that the ways in which one could demonstrate it in the context of the child/adult and lay/religious power relations of the early Seventies' convent-grammar-school required subtle and sullen and mostly silent negotiation. Negotiating the poem from such natural contrariness inevitably engendered a kind of suspicion. I became suspicious of the hushed, almost holy tones of the voice in which it tended to be read. That tone usually fronted a kind of authority dressed in reverence and respect: an authority whose very word was non-negotiable. And the final line of the poem – 'A four-foot box, a foot for every year' – brought the sad, pitiful and pious tone in which the rest of the poem had been read to a final crescendo. There didn't seem to me to be any way in which one could dare to criticise the poem without appearing callous, unsympathetic or even downright insolent. To find fault with it would have been an impertinence, like sniggering in church. 'Mid Term Break', it seemed, was a poem which was 'easy [for adults] to like'[40] and therefore difficult for the student not to like and therefore to criticise. So the criticism remained unvoiced, internal. Yet inside the reader, 'there was obviously an immense disparity between the finicky criticism I was conducting on the poem and the heavy price, in terms of emotional and physical suffering, the poet paid in order to bring it into being'.[41] But did the child have any correlative in terms of an equivalent emotional experience out of which to hear Heaney's poem?

One night, when I was nine or ten years old, I was awakened by the urgent, sobbing whispers of my mother as she roused my oldest sister to get up and go with her down the road to my granny's house where my aunt's three-month old baby had just died. I lay there in the dark, not letting on that I had heard the news. My reaction – which, in retrospect, may have been a defence against the fear I felt at the intense emotion in my mother's voice, as well as the fact that I had never seen this baby – was to think to myself, 'So what? It's only a baby. It's only been around for three months. It doesn't really know anybody. It has hardly lived at all, so what matter if it dies?' In retrospect, however, despite its apparent callousness, I am glad that the moment has stayed in my memory. It serves to illuminate a state of affairs in which adults may use a poem – albeit with the most honourable of intentions – to 'teach' children feelings. But the feelings they try to teach are feelings which a poem evokes in adults and are not necessarily the real feelings evoked in children by the same poem. This was certainly the case as far as 'Mid-Term Break' was concerned. I did not like the poem because I could not feel 'authentic feelings' in its presence. I suspected that I should feel sad and full of sympathy for the boy who had lost his little brother. But I didn't.

The best I could do was to pretend I did. This pretence made me feel uncomfortable. My discomfort irritated me and I 'took it out' on the poem. I was particularly angry with the last line: in my state of false feeling, the last line sounded to me like something out of the chorus of a country and western song, the kind Johnny Cash was singing on the records my older brothers and sisters had or the kind of line I would hear Big Tom sing some years later at Saturday night dances in Ardboe hall. Those hallowed tones in which the poem was spoken, as well as what I call the 'Everybody-say-"Ah"-factor' in the last line, blocked me from the blunt truth of the poem which I only became aware of when I read it again recently. The truth is, of course, that the speaker in the poem is entirely authentic in his feelings – or rather his numbness or none-ness of feeling, reflected in those matter-of-fact descriptions, line by line and step by step, of events as they occurred to him. Depths of feeling reside in the adults in the situation – the father crying, the mother's 'angry tearless sighs'.[42] The only 'feeling' word used in the whole poem is 'embarrassed', which is much closer to what I as a child felt in the face of adult emotion surrounding the poem. Of course all of this is the recollected experience of the young reader. What was, in fact, the reality, may have been quite different. But it does remain a fact that my initial encounter with the poetry of Seamus Heaney made little impression on me.

I was not aware until much later that Heaney had written anything other than poems – indeed that he had written anything other than 'Mid-Term Break'! But during the poetry course we were directed to read *Preoccupations* and I borrowed it from the library. I began to read. It was in Heaney's prose that I found a live connection: 'What was being experienced was not some hygienic and self-aware pleasure of the text but a primitive delight in finding world become word. I had been hungry for this kind of thing without knowing what it was I was hungering after.'[43] In this first contact with Heaney's prose writing I found 'the switch that sends writing energy sizzling into a hitherto unwriting system.'[44] In *Preoccupations*, especially the sections 'Mossbawn', 'Belfast', and 'Feeling into Words', were not only the world becoming word for me, but in an intimate way, the word becoming flesh – one's own flesh. Reflecting on why these writings made such an impact on me, is something which is best facilitated, not by looking directly on the experience of reading the book, but like Perseus, by looking at its reflection.

Once, at the age of eleven or twelve, I chanced upon another book which engrossed me as *Preoccupations* had done.   This book was hidden in the recesses of my mother's handbag.   It was a book explaining the facts of life – all news to me then. I devoured its contents. They were a revelation, a kind of private, secret uncovering, revealing a hidden (or more accurately, as yet forbidden) knowledge of the self to the self, as well as being something to revel in.   These opening chapters of *Preoccupations* were facts of a different kind – of life itself. One book I read crouched in the privacy of a locked bedroom, the other crouched in the quiet seclusion of a public library, like Heaney hiding in the fork of the beech tree or the throat of the old willow.   In 'that tight cleft'[45] I, too, was 'at the heart of a different life, looking out on the familar . . . as if it were suddenly behind a pane of strangeness.'[46]   And again, 'I didn't care who thought what about it: somehow, it had surprised me by coming out with a stance and idea that I would stand over.'[47] These two mirroring experiences became a 'sexual metaphor, an emblem of initiation, like putting your hand into the bush or robbing the nest, one of the various natural analogies for uncovering and touching the hidden thing.'[48] As I read through the pages, I became aware in myself that, whether I could do it or not, 'perhaps I could do this poetry thing too.'[49] The result of Heaney's – and of significant others' – influence on my work, has been a desire to assist children in making the same discovery in themselves.

[1]   Seamus Heaney, 'Casting and Gathering', *Seeing Things* (London: Faber,1991), p.13.

[2]   Seamus Heaney, *An Open Letter* (Londonderry: Field Day Theatre, 1983).

[3]   Seamus Heaney, *Preoccupations: Selected Prose 1968-1978,* (London: Faber, 1980), p.26.

[4]   *ibid,* p.45.

[5]   Sean O'Riordan, *Brosna* (Dublin: Sairséal and Dill, 1964) p.26.

[6]   *Preoccupations,* pp.47,48.

7   *English for ages 5 to 11* [the first Cox Report]. Department of Education and Science (London: DES, 1988), Chapter 10.19, p.48.

8   *An Open Letter.*

9   *Preoccupations,* p.45.

10 'Crossings' xxix, 'Squarings', *Seeing Things* (London: Faber, 1991), p.87.

11 'The Pulse', *Seeing Things,* p.11.

12 *ibid,* p.10.

13 'A Haul', *ibid.,* p.12.

14 *ibid.,* p.17.

15 *ibid.,* p.14.

16 Seamus Heaney, *The Government of the Tongue* (London: Faber, 1988), p.93.

17 *Problème du style,* p.69, quoted by Gertrude Patterson, *T. S .Eliot: Poems in the Making,* (Manchester: Manchester University Press, 1971), p.24.

18 T. E. Hulme, *Notes on Language and Style,* quoted by Gertrude Patterson, *ibid.*

19 T. S. Eliot, 'Hamlet', *Selected Essays* (London: Faber, 1951), p.145.

20 *The Government of the Tongue,* p. 47.

21 *Preoccupations,* p.45.

22 'Crossings' xl, 'Squarings', *Seeing Things,* p.100.

23 Seamus Heaney, Foreword to *Lifelines: Letters from Famous People about their Favourite Poem,* edited by Niall MacMonagle (Dublin:Tower House, 1992), p.xi.

24 *Preoccupations,* p.27.

25 'Imagisme', from *Poetry*, March 1913, reprinted in *Imagist Poetry,* edited by Peter Jones (Harmondsworth: Penguin, 1972), p.129.

26 Ted Hughes, *Poetry in the Making* (London: Faber, 1967), p.23.

27 Published in *Telepoems: The Biggest Poetry Competition Ever* (Dublin: The Ark, A Cultural Centre for Children,1995).

28 *English for ages 5-11,* 10.14, p. 47. See also 2.5.

29 Philip Wheelwright, *Metaphor & Reality* (Bloomington: Indiana University Press, 1975), p.81.

30 *Preoccupations,* p.41.

31 *ibid.*

32 *ibid.*, p.20.
33 Seamus Heaney, *Wintering Out* (London: Faber,1972), p.16.
34 Seamus Heaney, *Door into the Dark* (London: Faber,1969),
    p.37.
35 *Preoccupations*, p.45.
36 Patrick Kavanagh, 'Innishkeen Road: July Evening',
    Collected Poems (London: Martin Brian and O'Keefe,1972),
    p.17.
37 *Preoccupations*, p.44.
38 *ibid.*, p.54.
39 *The Government of the Tongue*, p.57.
40 *ibid.*, p.xv.
41 *ibid.*, pp.xv, xvi.
42 Seamus Heaney, *Death of a Naturalist* (London: Faber, 1966),
    p.28.
43 *The Government of the Tongue*, p.8.
44 *ibid.*
45 *Preoccupations*, p.18.
46 *ibid.*
47 *ibid.*, pp.41,42.
48 *ibid.*
49 *ibid.*

Poems

WORDS ARE HOPEFUL

Words can whirl and weave
Like mist, ribbons and kite,
Some are loose and free,
Swift and wild and run,
There are those that drip,
Soak, leak and damp,
And others are mysterious,
Like gloom and silhouette.
Words are sometimes fast,
Flash, zoom and rush,
And there are words that tire,
Dreary and droop and flop,
Sometimes words are hopeful,
Like maybe, sometime or soon
But some words have no end,
Eternity . . .
Farewell.

Claire, P5

READY STEADY NO

Can you jump into a poem
Like you jump into a pool
Or do you sit on the edge
And dabble your words
A toe or two at a time?

Catriona, 3rd Class

POEM SWITCH

I grope for a poem switch
In my head
But it's all dark in there
I can't find the light
To write.

Grace, 6th Class

POEM MAKING

I soloed
I dodged
I aimed
I kicked
I watched,
breathless
. . . . WIDE

Darragh, 4th Class

STICKY POETRY

It's stuck to my jumper like fluff;
Poetry is strange sorta stuff;
It's stuck like a tat in my hair -
However it got tangled up there,
It's stuck to my fingers like jam,
And I'm licking it still, so I am,
And it's stuck like a fly in my eye,
And it's making it water and cry;
It's stuck on my knee like the grime
Of the plaster's left-over black line,
It's stuck on my tongue like a hair,
That came from-
I don't know where,

So where does poetry come from?

5th, 6th Class

TRYING IT ON

One day I made myself a poem.
I tried it on.
I looked in the mirra.
The buttons were done up
Wrong.

Grace, 2nd Class

POETRY AND PROSE

Prose blows
flows of bubbles
into the air, where
they burst their insides out.

Poetry reverses the flow
motion, distilling bubbles
in liquid
potential
the wand
in your hand.

Clare (teacher)

PAINTING

paintbrush tickles page
until hole giggles
its way through painting
wetting itself with
the laughing.

Clare (teacher)

TOFFEE POETRY

I bite into the hard toffee
Of my poem's unyielding
Awkwardness
In my mouth,
Can't get my tongue
Around this poem.
Jaws clench
Fingers tense
Words stick
In my teeth.

Pen pokes
To free the sticky toffee
More malleable now
I chew it over
Mmm! I like it
And swallow.

Maria, 6th Class

Trying to Cycle a Bike

I pedal an idea
Round and round
In my head.

I try to steer it
Along.

Words
Spokes
Pencils
Verses
Spinning, spinning, spinning.
Round and round
On my page
My poem
Getting nowhere fast.

David, 6th Class

Which one should I choose?

Some words are enemies like
Cat and Dog.
Some make me cough
Like Smoke and Smog.
Some are burrowing like
Tunnel and Deep.

And some are curious like
Sneaky and Peep.

Some are destructive
Tornado, Explode.
Some are complicated
Computer Mode.

Some are murky like
Cave or Castle.
Some are rude like
'You little rascal'.

These words are mine
All mine to use.
So I ask you this question -
Which one should I choose?

Pamela, P5

HIDEOUT

I live beside a
Field of ideas.

I made a poem hut there
Out of words and branches and twigs.

There are cows wondering
In my field of ideas.

Cows knock
My poem hut down.

They think my field of ideas
Is theirs to eat.

Cows don't understand my poetry.

Ruth, 4th Class

WEDNESDAY

On each attentive ear fall her slow, soft vowels.
Tentatively teasing out our halting clumsy responses,
She patiently threads her way
Through the silence of our
Inadequacy.
Outside, the early winter green of the cherry
Struggles to calm its vigorous impulse
Prematurely to unfurl its white confetti.
Inside, we slowly make our way through metaphor and symbol,
Faltering in the greyness of the twilight hour,
We launch our apprehensive search
Through the terrain of words,
Landscaped with love's labour by the poet and craftsman.
Here we dig over their symbolic patterns,
Delving each deep furrow,
Harvesting the crafted image.
Each reader's liberated consciousness,
A glimpsed discovery of poets and the poet's vocation.
Outside, the white spray of the cherry tree,
Bursting from its darkness,
Initiates a solemn moment of its own fulfilment.

Eileen (teacher)

LY-CRO LANGUAGE

Lycra language stretches
To fit precisely
What a body needs to say.
No sagging of the bottom
Line, or bagging at the knees,
Or droopy jowled vowels, tongue-in cheek.
It has plenty of give
To let the voice breathe
In and out without fear
Or falling apart at the seams.

Velcro-speak fastens meaning in place
For as long as needs be
Bound to society.
But snitched asunder
What words have joined together,
Lips part, and the mouth is free
To shout it
Or shut it - quietly.

Clare (teacher)

INTERIOR DECORATING AN ART NOUVEAU

I'm bending here
Over the dado rail
And praying it will go on properly.

Like an amateur weightlifter
Steeled, nervously perspirant
I approach the idea.

With an inward rush of air
And a snatch
It is off the ground
And just below my line of sight
On the paper.

Staggering steps
Take an unstable burden
To the wall.

Patiently,
Pastel green with ideas
The paper and paint
Wait,
Steady in reception.
But beginnings and endings
Wobble uncertainly in the air.

Set against the reality of the wall
The first touches on paper
Steady me
And lessen the tremors.

The pine settles at an angle
A little elevation
And correction
There
Slight but not
Insignificant.
That seems better
But am I too close?
The setting pins of draft and
Others' view
Allow reflection.

And give a chance
To step back
Into perspective.

We are set
For the first nail of type
Levelled,
Steadied
Silvered, like treasure,
With the gentle tap of
Perseverance, it is in.
Confirmed idea
Gives steadier hold,
I tap along its length
Towards the end.
Furrowed brow,
Quiet hammering,
Nails held in lips,
A stream of action.

And finally,
Silently,

It is there.
The task completed.

Another minor element
On a sparkling,
Smiling
Spring Saturday afternoon.

Martin, (teacher)

THE ARGOS CATALOGUE

Imagine an Argos Catalogue
Of 'Poems and Rhymes'
All for something pounds
Ninety-nine.
(a poetic bargain)

Ciara, 6th Class

THE WORM

Baby sparrows, necks taut, skin stretched,
Like the old man's pinched cheek,
With bulging eyes, trapped tadpoles
Under pink skin
Strain and plead to the mother bird
For vital food: the worm.
The small child
Strains upwards, sparrow-like, to hear,
Mouths open wide to catch each syllable.
Too often what we feed are
Soft and squelchy,
The sickly sweets of sentimental rhyme.
With little wonder then
The worm turns.

Jennifer (teacher)

BOREDOM

Boring is when you're fed up
Boring is when you've nothing to do
Boring is when you've no one to play with
Boring is the tin of biscuits when the fancy ones are all eaten
Boring is when the ball won't bounce
Boring is Sunday afternoon when the grown-ups sleep with the

papers
Boring is when the fizz is all out of the Coke
Boring is Daniel O'Donnell on Top of the Pops.

3rd, 4th Class

MY CLASS

Like a bag of jelly babies
They squash together
Without choice.
Their different colours a hint of individuality.
Sometimes I want to savour them
Sucking their different flavours out.
Other times I feel like
Viciously
Biting their heads off!

Susan (teacher)

OUT

Work may be out
But what use is a burnt out
Barrrel of broken grey ash?
Take it out on the beer mat.
Trace intricate froth cobwebs
That repeat on the rim.

Stare lifeless at fingertips
That death march on glass.

In the swirling brown depths
Is a smoulder.
Conviviality, familiarity tease out
A being, other than the clone
Who masquerades week-long.
A passion burns within:
Break free from belt.
Fires flame and fancy,
Not ash.
I am what I should be,
Briefly.

Barbara (teacher)

RELEASE

Silent and inarticulate
In a corner, neglected, voiceless,
Rosewood and gut held speechless.

Tense and ready
It stirs to sing.

The horsehair loosens
The voice of strings,
The air floods
Mellifluous and honey-toned.
The player, thus engrossed,
Weaves sonorous melody
Transforming tunelessness to soothing harmony.

Claire (lecturer)

AWAKENING

Fresh from his bed, the pocket-sized adventurer
Bursts forth into his new domain.
Toys scatter and the raft is readied,
As captain, conqueror and teddy put to sea.
The wearied parents groan and turn in bed,
As pioneer scales patterned mounds.
Traipsing and tripping, so much to explore
When down he tumbles on the canyon floor.

Returning to the raft, the pilfering fists
Hoard buttons, keys, and pennies,
A treasure safely stowed on board.

The voyager casts off, the immobile cruise begins,
As captain ventures forth to frontiers new.

Claire (lecturer)

IN THE CITY PARK

It's Saturday afternoon
In the city park.

The trees are inside out
Fine thin lines, pencil-drawn against
The greyness of the winter sky.
Rough ends of brown tangled threads
And knots of joins,
Reaching high
Or drooping low
Twigs transfixed.
And waiting.

A black litter bin stands full
Between two empty benches.

Three dozen pigeons glide
And land
Beneath the bare branches
Busy fat bodies strutting
Heads down
Tails up
Sewing machines
Stitching the ground.
One struts over to the pathway.
His tiny head sinks in his fat, purple chest.
His orange eye with bright, black dot.
Head jerks, eyes flick,
He moves busily.

The pigeons warble with low bubbling sounds.
A female voice blares from a transistor radio.

A crow caws.

Disparate sounds in the cold air.
Outside the railings,
In the traffic rush
Red city buses pass in the wash of sound
Move on.
No waiting here.

Withered leaves curl, splashing patterns over the trodden grass.
A shabby flag moves briefly on a red-brick building.
Birds chatter.
A small woman hunched in sugar pink anorak
Clutches a dark purple shopping bag in one hand
And pulls a large, scrawny dog.
Strong spruce trunks with peeling bark
Snakes wrestling on a canvas.
Strollers pass.
An old man in grey trilby
And dark glasses, walks briskly.
A boy with rucksack and a white peaked cap,

Riding a bicycle
Through the city park.

The chipped green paint on   railings
Fences a corner under the spruce tree,
Where tiny crocuses bloom purple and gold.

The threads of images,
Bare lines of trees,
The busy pigeons -
Colour in the wastes of the cold city

Putting threads together,
Unravelling knots,
On Saturday afternoon
In the city park.

Maire (teacher)

OUR ENVIRONMENT

In the stream trout dart along,
In a tree a starling's song,
In the air I feel the breeze,
To-day is cold, the night will freeze.
On suburb walls you read graffiti,
Bent lamp-posts lean within the city.
But here there is the tractor's sound,
The howling of a basset hound,
Along the coast the crash of sea –
Our country is the place for me.

Robert, P 6

THE WAGON

The Lagan flows gracefully
Like a wagon

Past Dromore, Dromara
More and more,
From Slieve Croob to the sea.
(Where I like to be)
There, robbed of her glory
The end of her story.

Ross, P4

INIS OIRR

Steeped in its history and its culture
Gaelic in tongue and flavour,
This unfarmable island
Floats like paradise
Mid-Atlantic, West of Doolin, County Clare.

High on O'Brien's Castle
The whole island can be seen,
From the barren rock of the west,
To the long shore on the east,
Dry stone walls stretched in front of you
Divide the land: a hundred patchwork fields.

My roots lie deep
In this Atlantic island
Grandfather, Great-Grandfather and
Fathers before them,
Buried low in sandy graves
Which face the sea.
The only sounds uninterrupted silence
This bit of Heaven and a special place for me
I have walked where you walked,
Sung where you sang
Sat where you sat,
And each time thought of you.
I comprehend your leaving
But not your failure to return

To this, the island of your youth,
Where patchwork fields
Roll silent to the sea.

Magnetic pull of time
Which generations later
Continues to draw me.

Otteran (teacher)

BANGOR BAY

Bangor Bay is a never-ceasing tongue
Licking its way up the shingle and the shimmering sand;
Spume and surf float on the foamy depths,
Jostling to touch the tide-line first.
Seaweed and pebbles toss up on the beach,
And relics of dry, twisted driftwood,
The invigorating wind whispers with the waves,
Driving the gulls over the lighthouse,
Warning the ships to sail clear,
While Bangor sleeps on.

Ellen, P6

YOU CHOOSE

Would you live in Stabannon
if you had the choice?

There's the school for the children
There's the pub for the men,
There's the church for the women,
There's the youth-club for in-between,
And then there's Richard,
Stabannon's main man.
Richard holds his head high,
Just to show that Richard can,

Richard smokes in your face,
Flicks his ash with such grace,
Richard smiles down the aisle from Communion.

Would you live in Stabannon
if you had the choice?

Brid, 5th Class

GILFORD

The old mill stands like a speechless giant
His red brick chest bravely sprayed by vandals;
Redundant for many years
But hopeful that he may work again.
Terraced houses nestle in the giant's shadow,
Dilapidated buildings newly restored,
Stony cobbles peep through cracks in the concrete,
As the River Bann weaves its way in and out the town:
Gilford the old stumbles towards its rebirth.

Gareth, P7

BANGOR BAY

The sea ripples and ebbs
The luminous moonlight reflecting on the water;
Waves drift timelessly,
Dark shadows lurk under the depths of the sea,
The fluffy foam rests peacefully on the shoreline
As the sea laps the sand with its big curling tongue.
Sea smothers the rocks beneath,
And the lighthouse blinks restlessly.

Aaron, P6

Twilight in Bangor

Dusk falls over Bangor
Waves lap upon the shore;
The rumble of the Crawfordsburn train heard in the distance,
Like some huge, angry prowling animal.
A light film of mist falls across the bay,
A lonely crab scuttles out on the sand,
A few gulls wheel above squawking
Like banshees,
As the fishing trawlers drift in.

Joanne, P5

Bangor Bay

Sea is a monster
A fearless terrible monster,
Snarling, swallowing sand and shingle,
Splashing, pounding ships in harbour.
Sheltering crabs
Scuttle to and fro;
White horses ride the
Waves in Bangor Bay.

Michael, P6

Ballydougan Townland

The twisted lanes of Ballydougan
Swirl and slide
Through the gentle townland.
The mass of trees
Line the roadside,
Like elderly women
Arching their backs
To the juicy gossip

Of their neighbouring kind.
The ruined barn, its
Crumbled walls and shattered windows,
Reminders now of what held harvest sturdily.
The marshy fields
Like huge mud monsters,
Slushing and gurgling,
Protect their territory.

Christopher, P 7

SUNLIGHT ON NEWCASTLE

The sunlight shines over Newcastle
It makes you feel welcome here.
The trees are green, golden and rust.
When I was up on Drinnahilly at the mast,
I would have loved to swoop like a bird
And fly over the blue carpet of sea.

Naomh, P4

THE MOUNTAINS OF MOURNE IN WINTER

Slieve Donard's a giant with snow on his head,
Beside little Thomas with no snow at all,
And the Blackstairs frozen stiff
There is Commedagh with plenty of snow
And Drumakilly with trees of rust and green.
As the sun moves, the shadows come and go,
The quarry is gleaming and glooming.
Bang! - there goes an explosion,
See the dust and a puff of smoke,
(For men need granite to make our footpaths.)
Between Commedagh and Donard
A valley lies.
It's called the Saddle
Can you guess why?

Clare, P4

MY STREET

There's Dympna Cunningham craning her ears,
There's Helana Wallace trying to soothe her baby,
The diggers, the diggers are making a row!
Get off the road, the diggers are coming!
Bikes race off the road,
Children give a piercing cry and scatter,
The diggers rumble past,
Dympna Cunningham takes her hands from her ears,
Helena Wallace's baby stops crying,
Till the next digger comes by.

Helen, P4

THE MOURNE MOUNTAINS

From our school yard
I can see Slieve Donard
And little Thomas too.
He sits before Big Donard
Like father and son.
I can see Commedagh
Beside Slieve Donard;
They've got a valley between them
Like a saddle.
I can see Drinanahilly
With Mr Mast on top,
With his metal legs
And his twisted head.
Further down are the trees,
Dark brown and russet
Where they have been cut down.
And below all that, the green sea.

Helen, P5

OUR SCHOOL YARD

Black headed gulls come every day
To our school yard.
They're our dustmen,
For they pick up all our rubbish.
Their uniform is not green like ours -
It's white with a dark brown cap.
But in winter they leave off their caps
                    Silly birds !
And wear their Walkmans instead.

Roisin, P5

THE VIEW FROM OUR SCHOOL

Standing in the playground
I can see Slieve Donard, the mountain,
With Thomas, his son.
Just near, the valley Blackstairs is flowing.
Every time I see the Saddle,
I wonder if it gets its name from Finn McCool.
Did he ride the mountains like a horse
And flatten out the valley in between?
Up from the Saddle is Mummy Commedagh,
Swooping down to meet Slieve Donard.
There they stand, hand in hand,
Looking down over the school.

Siobhan, P4

ONCE UPON A TIME

Once upon a time . . . there lived deceit.
It stalked the dark streets,
A monster of a divided town.
After sectarian, bloody deeds,

It speaks placatory, lying tones,
'We're not a divided people,
Ours is a close community',
The Mayor smiled,
'We all live happily here.'
He's old though,
His practising, appeasing tongue
Forgets the fairy-tale
'Happily ever after.'
Where deceit spills out its hatred on a street corner,
To-morrow and to-morrow the platitudes continue,
And seek to camouflage the truth,
While we, retreating to our streets,
Continue together,
And live apart.

Amanda, Year 3 FE

STREETS APART

The terraced houses sleep uneasily,
Under the smouldering smog of sullen Belfast sky.
Back to back they closely lie,
Like pairings of soured marriage beds.
Consuming bitterness engulfs
Division's silence, tearing each apart.
Their enmity increases like a cancer,
Hurts well past healing's reconciliation.
Irretrievably broken down,
A marriage and a street.

Denise, Year 1 FE

SHAKY TOOTH

A shaky tooth
And a pushy tongue
Just cannot leave

Each other alone.
It's coming . . . coming
Coming . . . OUT!
It's all red.

I thought it was white.

Tara, 3rd Class

BUTTERFLIES

Flying through the air,
Lovely clouds to share,
Used to fly and now still will.
Tears of glitter.
Tipping of pitter
Even if it stops.
Really tender,
Flying through the night.

Victoria, P4

Fly around my garden all morning and night,
Lift your wings to the morning light
And slow them down at night.
Up you fly
To the tree above,
Tender wings.
Eat up now,
Red leaves in the late autumn sky.

Ryan, P4

LOUGH NEAGH VILLAGE

Like a ghost at sea,
The moon shimmers across the lough,

And comes to rest on the village.
Bordered by nonchalant, twisty roads,
The houses huddle close,
Embracing silence.
The pact of years
Have strengthened their resolve to stay unmoved.
Rows of tidy gardens,
Bordering their domesticity,
Measure in perennial blooms
The passing of the seasons,
And the years.
Here a community breathes out,
Pulsates behind the red brick terraces,
Lace-curtained, resilient to change, they stand
Firm to the purpose of their no-surrenders,
And suffocate in darkness.

Susan, Year 4 FE

SWIMMING IN POETRY

A smooth watered pool
Like a clean new page
Inviting me in,
Inviting my pen
To swim.
Pity to sully the waters
With awkward words
And phrases;
But how else to know
If my poem will sink or swim.

Kim, 4th Class

THE LAMBEG DRUM

The rhythm of the drums
Vibrant in the morning of July,

Beat assertion's
Territorial claim
To the rich Ulster soil.
My father,
The strap already stinging on his neck,
Like an expectant mother,
Carries the Lambeg
'All to the front'.
The furious blasts assault my ears,
Then silence,
A sacramental stillness,
Before the beats again rise vehement,
The labour of a new tune being born.

Scott, Year 4 FE

THE TWELFTH -DAY PARADE

The procession curls its way
Through the long line of spectators,
The pageant boldly announcing
This day belongs to us.
Coloured banners tug the morning air,
And the thump of drums,
The rhythm of Protestantism,
Resounds through the streets.
Collaretted, the marching brethren
Step out in symmetrical remembrance
Of a river, a battle, and a king.

Sonya, Year 3 FE

TO PHIL COULTER

You who wrote the song,
You are wrong.
Your romantic chords pluck a nostalgia
Which groans from the past,

Misrepresented and distorted.
Your indulgent 'Derry Air',
Languishing in the homely street scene,
And the early morning mists
Discredit our people.
The freshly dug graves of innocents
Refute your music,
Lilting over the screaming God-forsaken hills.
You dare make music
When orphans cry?

John, Year 3 FE

SPRING IS

-       Taking off your shoes and socks to race in the grass
-       Smelling the newly cut lawn
-       Tying your jumper around your waist
-       White legs and arms
-       Not many swans left on the bog
-       The feeling to go for a walk
-       First time you take your bike instead of the school bus
-       Salad instead of hot dinner
-       Not noticing that the fire's out.

3rd, 4th Class

AUTUMN

Summer gone rusty,
Bleak and withered,
Trees having a snooze until spring
Wakens them up.
Leaves huddle together for warmth,
Old and wrinkled soon to die.
Desolate,
Lonely,
Menacingly calm,
The wind whistles on,

The corn sways to its lullaby.
The leaves die,
Chestnuts lie helpless on the ground,
Delighted hands scoop them up.
Red berries sway perpetually staring
At the ground,
Until some robin redbreast neatly picks them off.

Sharon, P7

WINTER

Snow on parked cars.
Snow on the ground,
Snowdrifts against trees and walls.
Later, the sound of wheels
Driving through dirty slush,
Feet trudging in mush,
Robins eating from the frozen bird table,
And big black crows dotted
Along telephone wires

Patrick, P5

THE PEACOCK

Peacock is blooming
Showing colours gracefully,
Like Spanish dancers.

Sharon, P7

INCISION

Massive Ferguson
unzips the chest of the hill;
gulls like white corpuscles
spill into the sky.

Clare (teacher)

In Tollymore Forest

Snowdrops appear every spring
Their stems as thick as cord
And greener than the leaves on the tree.
Petals white as milk
And smooth like silk.
Snowdrops white as the water lilies
Float on the pond under the trees
In Tollymore Forest Park.

Paula, P5

Jack Frost

Jack Frost was in the garden
I saw him there at dawn
He was dancing round the bushes
And prancing on the lawn.
He had a cloak of silver
A hat all shimmering white
A wand of glittering star dust,
And shoes of sunbeam light.

John, P3

My lady Spring

My lady Spring is dressed in green
She wears a yellow crown
And little baby buds and twigs
Are clinging to her gown.

Matthew, P3

OCTOBER'S PARTY

October gave a party
The leaves by hundreds came
The chestnuts, oaks and maples
And leaves by every name.
The sunshine spread the carpet
And everything was grand,
Miss Weather led the dancing
Professor Wind the band.

Cormac, P4

TREE

As former Eves we two have sat
And eyed a different tree with fruit
No sounder, and still all the same
Without appeal.
This is the sullen piece which I adore
In a cream bowl stood along the edge
Of off-balance, skeletal, silver cast,
From rattling- can, its silhouette
Still burnished coolly on the concrete
Where it was once adorned. Steely negative,
After-image of this capricious craft.

Lean sister, amply clad in monochrome
With arabesque of silvered limbs
Gesticulating to me plainly
Through a froth of sibilant mousse.
Elite syncopations of its soft percussions,
A glockenspiel of season's craft.

In the shadow of the bookcase
White winter sun bulbs, yellowing by day
And we two sitting pale-faced
In its greying glade.

Across the room the light through slats
Blinds and fails again,
And Eve upon Eve comes to mind
Until the tardy chore dismantling her
Inevitable.

So, snapping underfoot with brutish hands
Each striving arm dismembered
Into the black bag thrust,
Swollen, unseeming, with
My tree, this icon now deranged.

One watchful remnant now retrieved,
And properly asymmetrical,
Flexing wayward sand
With glassy charm, hung, solo.

There beside the portrait of Christ,
See! fittingly troubled.
Wearied about the brow, reddening
Stirred by the icy icon. Dead?
Observe the green grey leaf,
Its only foliage. Angel with grey face.
Modigliani's Heaven.

Bernadette, (teacher)

POOR ME

Poor me
Poor me
It's always the same
I wanted it fancy
It ended up plain.

Poor me
Poor me

It's terribly sad
For when I'm without it
It drives me quite mad.

Brid, 5th class

MY NAME

'Sarah' is for basic me
And the things about me you can always see.
'Esmeralda' is for fantasy me,
And all the things I'd like to be.
'Ursula' is an awful me, I wish she was a 'you',
She's prissy and she's practical and super tidy too.
'Jessica' is flighty, dancey,   absolutely useless me,
I like being her a lot,
She knocks down things around the house and
breaks the baby's cot.
'Josephine''s weird wacky me,
I think she's frankly crazy,
'Jane''s my reading, writing me,
 And interrupted, she's a cow,

But she's the one I like being now.

Josephine Jane, 1st Year

GRANNY

My granny has marble eyes
She's a slipper -walker.

Michael, P1

MY GRANNY

My Granny stumps about on swollen legs,
Kind eyes hidden in her wrinkled face,
Her arms outstretched to hug and hold.
But underneath her smiles I think she's sad.
She quarrels with my Mum about my Dad,
And then alone,
In her big chair upstairs,
Her worried lines relax
And dreams comes back
Of her lost son, a boy like me.

Robert, P5

STORY TELLING

and
and he . . .
and
and she. . .
and
and when . . .
and
and so . . .
and
and yet . . .
and
and on and on . . .
and grows . . .
and then

the end!

Group poem

THE RIGHT THING

When going to write
I wanted to wear
Clothes just right for the occasion
Something loose and meaningful
To keep me cool in the heat of the writing
Something colourful, bright, light, right, and airy
 - I just can't decide . .

Simon, 1st Year

FOR A STUDENT'S CHILDREN

I see you go, in other directions
Down through the wet grass on Sundays
At a time - afternoon - when families
When couples, when children -
Through the garden gate and out, I see you go.

The house, as suddenly emptied, settles around me
And once again time opens fresh as a box of pencils
And once there is possibly
(You whom I love in your absences)
A way forward (as your outward footprints track
my page);
Eased of you as after a long labour
Myself again, flat-bellied, taut, knit to my own
purposes,
I sit behind glass
At a table with yellow chrysanthemums.

Silence comes that is not ringed and rippled
With your voices, but pooled for deep fishing.
You are here to reproach me,
I breathe out as once, tiptoeing from your rooms
Nightly with fingers crossed I breathed,
Gambled for time and lost with a bad grace.

Older, you expect less but look angrier
As others, mothers, pack thermos flasks,
Sandwich in outings, Sundays, when couples
When parents, when families -

Yet how will you know that I love you now
Unless seeking the word that will truly draw
Your mackintoshed backs departing
I can let you go.

Eileen,(teacher)

GRAMMAR OF LIFE

I am hungry
You are hungry
He is hungry
She is hungry
We are hungry
You are hungry
They are hungry

5th, 6th Class,

LIVING ROOM

I was watching the telly
And on came the news
I saw these black children,
No food, no clothes, no shoes.
I thought, 'This is awful
I'll put a stop to that.'
I went in to the telly
Made a friend,
Had a chat.

'Come on out here
To my living room with me

You can share some of my clothes
And I'll give you your tea.
I'm sure my jeans would fit you
And my other runners - size two,
And sausage, beans and chips for tea
Will that be O.K. for you?'

'What's your name?
Where do you live?
Where do you go to school?
Who's your best friend?
When is your birthday ?
Would you like to go to the pool?
Do you like Michael Jackson?
Did you see 'Home Alone'?
What age are your brothers and sisters?
Have you also got a bike of your own?
Isn't it better living here?
Sure stay ...Why not?. . .For Good!'

But she only said in a whispery voice
'I want to go home'.

3rd,4th Class

THE TRANSACTION

He lies,
'At peace', they say.
The heavy sweetness of the flowers which scent the room
Nauseates and overwhelms with dread.
Strangers fill the corners, whisper respectful platitudes,
Painfully they smile and bid goodbye,
Escaping the embarrassed darkness.
Newcomers re-invade the corners,
Sympathetic, curious,
Hear our story,
Nod their well-rehearsed response,

'It's a terrible business', they mumble.
Shaking hands
Sincerity is sealed.
Their duty done,
They too return to other worlds outside.

Inside once more,
Our silences return
And speak our grief in quieter tones.

Gareth, Year 3, FE

MAUREEN'S

The world within this tight-shelved box has gone,
Its life-sustaining liquor oozed
Through widening cracks,
Exhaled completely now she's gone.

Remembering how flower-sleeved smock
She stood in search of clove rock, midget gems,
Unhurried, fingering through the leaf-worn book
of stamps,
Indexed with neat, curt snips of brown-edged
cornflake box.

Skeletal, rigged shelves wasted to bare board,
Which once were fat with well-fleshed fare,
Like muscled limbs, flexed, suspended harvests
Of rusted fruit tins, Fray Bentos, Plumrose,
bubblies, stale specked chocolate.
Prisms of sherbet, refracting blinks of winter
sunshine.

On peeling wall ranged ranks of Fluke drench,
Jeyes's Fluid, stiff brown paper, balls of string
Black boot wax, Kiwi, laces shouldering space alongside
                                        cigarettes:
Woodbine, Players, Raw Plug tobacco, chunks or ready rubbed

Astringent cleansing cure of Brasso, Lifebuoy,
Zoflora, Vim.

Beyond all that the beaded curtained doorway,
Hypnotically chimes Sesame to dark unfathomed space.
A private world, warm currants of her sister's baking
Commingled every breath of open door,
Which rasped against the hard unyielding , stone-flagged floor,
Of this most Presbyterian edifice.
A cold, yet life-sustaining blast of air
Announced arrival of each questing guest,
Tripartite – visitor, friend and customer in one,
To spend, and spending, spend an idle minute in 'The Shop'.

The wind keens loudly at the empty door,
While echoes snigger whispers of the many sounds within,
The thousand conversations of the life that's spent.

'Not a bad day that, there's drying in it.'
'It'll be no time now till the Twelfth.'
The talk of shows, the minister, the silage cut and
Cochrane's wake,
The latest tractor and the dreadful bane of youth
Ill-spent on discos, drugs and drink.

There's much beyond the sum of things we see,
A living housing spirit of the townland in its soul.
A way of life and commerce, giving way to brisk efficient,
Plate-glass, cut-price crowds, Hell-bent on finding fast and fresh,
Efficient, electronic, symmetrical and mowed,
Synthetic harvest of consumer greed for speed.
This shrouded box now mourns what's
Going, Going,
Gone.

Cathryn, (teacher)

DAN, DAN . . .

Big black bike
Leaning into our front-garden hedge,
Coat rolled up neatly, tied on the carrier
In case the rain comes on
Bulging bag of Merrymaids or
Riley's Chocolate Toffee Rolls for our
Big houseful
D'ye get me. . .?

Sitting at the kitchen table
Back against the curtain,
Legs crossed, big workin' boots
Laced up, but not to the very top,
In reverie, a pipe, a packet of Warhorse
And a box of
Swift matches slowly turning
Over and over between finger and thumb
Like an egg-timer
But time doesn't matter,
D'ye get me. . . ?

Every Christmas morning
Five bobs; two half-crowns all round,
Ten shilling notes for the two oldest,
Every Christmas dinner, a leg of the turkey
For Dan and Daddy, then the rest for us,
Then Mammy,
Every Christmas night
Away home his lone,
D'ye get me . . .?

Daddy's relative
But more akin to Mammy,
Talking away in the scullery with the door shut,
'I sent my mother a wheen a' pound. Well
She reared me didn't she?

D'ye get me . . .?
One thing we had in common with Christ,
They both were thirsty at the end,
(and a Mary there beside them too, waiting)
'I says to them in the hospital,
I'm no afeard to die.
I'll only do it once – am I right?
D'ye get me . . .?

No harm to you God,
But he'll want no mansion in your house
– Some wee place of his own
Up one of Heaven's lanes,
Across a couple of Heaven's fields, in a corner,
His mother to call once or twice,
– a whitewash job,
Maybe,
D'ye get me . . .?

'D'ye get me God?', he'll say
'D'ye get me now?'
God'll stifle a smile and say:
'I have ye , Dan,
'I have ye now,
Here,
Take a wee drink of this cup, man,
And you'll never be thirsty again,
D'ye get me . . .?

Clare (teacher)

PERSONAL ARCHAEOLOGY

Old skin has dried to flake and husk,
Hair sprouts and crinkles to a bush,
Bone curves out and forms a tusk,
And teeth project from malign use.

Behind the eyes, the cry of fear
Originates in horn and hoof,
Snorts, bellows, but still makes it clear,
That this is nature, red in tooth.

David (teacher)

WHAT IS WHITE?

White is a drop of wine, maybe the last,
White is the illness that still hasn't passed,
White is the snowdrop that falls on the grass
White is the Dove we remember in Mass.

Claire, P5

A LETTER TO GREY

Dear Grey,

Some people think of you as dirty, gloomy,
Evil colour.
But I think of you differently!

You're the fog, falling on the land
Hiding all the ugliness of man.
You're the rain clouds which helps Green
Grow his grass.
You're my Man. United away kit,
Encouraging my sporting abilities.
You're the fillings in my teeth,
Protecting them from bacteria,
And you're a shark
Gliding through blue, a silent predator.

I think you're
The King of colours . . . Grey!

Paul , P6

WHAT ARE . . . THE STARS?

Saints' eyes, looking down from Heaven,
Flying saucers, coming to invade our Earth,
Spies like flashing torches, keeping bright eyes out
for crooks and scoundrels.
Silver streaks appearing in the darkness of black hair,
Mini lampposts, lighting up the grey streets of the sky,
Or glittering white saucers on midnight's tablecloths.

Ryan, P5

BREAK!

'That's someone's cup!', an angry voice snaps off
The words that sting like blows across my cheek,
I redden,
Panic stricken like the child as I once was.
'Use one of those,' the voice adds, unmoving and unmoved,
A hand points, dismissive, like a claw,
All rings and chicken skin.
I limp and mumble lame and late contrition,
Retreat with cup in hand
To seek safe shelter in the pouring of the tea.

The cup now nestles in my hand,
Stared at like words of prayer,
Avoiding watchful eyes that smile benignly like conspirators,
And murder with a glance.
The silence has surrendered now,
To petty discourse which mercifully sidesteps me.
Cocooned, I slowly sip my tea,
Refit my cup back to its place,
And wait, for
Liberating bells to ring
The end of break
And freedom.

Michael (teacher)

MSR9

(Once upon a non-existent wrinkle)

When mornings were negotiable
and life was measured sociable
by unwashed coffee cups:

I masqueraded my dreams
in white-kneed jeans
trying to dodge
reality

and, worked so hard
at it that life distilled by degrees

Annetta (teacher)

SUM MASTER

Sum how
Sumtime
Sumwhere
Sumone or
Sumthing
Will tell the master to
Sum-up
(But not me!)

3rd, 4th Class

LOST AND FOUND

Even if they're found
They'll soon be lost again

- the keys of the car
- the baby's bottle

- Mammy's purse
- the remote control
- the scissors and sellotape

And found
- down the back of the sofa
- under the telly
- out in the car
- fallen into the coal bucket

- in the jam-jar behind the curtain on the kitchen   window
- in the bottom of my schoolbag

- where I left it.

3rd, 4th Class

TECHNIC-LY SPEAKING

Answering machine
Opened the door
C.D. said 'Hi! Fi!'
Fax relaxed with some micro-chips
So Micro waved 'bye-bye'.
She decided to go for a Walkman
Although she didn't N-intend to
Then she Fast-Tracked back
For a Mega Drive
Around to the Kar-y-out.
OK then?

Mark, 5th Class

THE EXTRA THINGS

The smell of mum's cooking on a winter night
And the misted kitchen window.
Newly cut grass baking in the sun

And the smell of my grandad's pipe.
The feel of fine sawdust running through my hand.
And the gentle lap of the warm waves.
The first breath of air on a frosty day
The unbroken surface of the lake,
The colourful rippling patterns on the wall
On an early sunlit day.
The sunset reflecting in the sky
And all the comforting sounds of life.

Claire, P6

UNBURDENED

The track is still there
Though it doesn't feel bare
Without my circular band

For love's broken token
With its heaviness all spoken
I've removed from my hand.

Like a jettisoned plane
Without the strain
Finds it lighter to land.

And the horse without traces
His freedom he faces
Can make his own stand.

The track is still there
Though it doesn't feel bare
To walk without a hand.

Rita (teacher)

CODED WARNING

Ignorant of cause, aware of effect,
the drivers sit in their lanes, silent,
as I pass, moving in the opposite direction,
vaguely worried for a loved one, ensnared,
probably, in the coils of the city streets.
Police cones, police men, and I,
driving out of Belfast on the M2,
northwards, viewing car after car,
van after van, row after row,
static, stationary, or edging forward, inch by inch.
I slow, perhaps in sympathy, perhaps to observe
the closer,
and notice, as I drive beneath a laden
flyover, dwarfed, below the juggernauts,
city bound, a tiny lorry, bearing Christmas trees.

Keith (teacher)

SUNT LACRIMAE RERUM

What did it feel like then
– the fall, the rapid descent?
Was there a moment, when you knew
what had happened?
And did you think,
have time to think in the rushing madness
of death?
And after, did you see a face,
recognise a friend, before withdrawing
helpless to the shades?

Or was it not like that
– but a sickening wrench,
a headlong scream, the dull and deadening thud?

I am not your father,

but when I think of you,
I feel like Daedalus,
as he stands, his heart filled with grief,
beside the sea called Icaria.

Keith (teacher)

THE PUPPET MAN

The puppet man with his puppet clan
Came to our school to-day.
He said, 'Well! Hello! Will you come to my show?'
He said 'Ready ! Steady! Let's go!

A wig and a hat, a joke and a chat,
A song and a clap and a bow;
There was laughter and after the water got squirted,
We giggled and sniggled, 'What now?'

Said Mark, 'What the heck 'bout a sword in the neck,
It's only a trick, so I'll try it!'
His laugh sounded hollow as he tried not to swallow,
Now all of a sudden he's quiet!

Behind the striped canvas, the puppets lay handless,
Awaiting their turn to impress us,
Which they did more and more and we shouted 'Encore!'
But he's gone with his puppets. God bless us!

(And them too.)

5th, 6th Class

Bibliography

BIBLIOGRAPHY

1: Primary Sources
A: Reports Consulted:

Half our Future [the Newsom Report]. Report of the Central Advisory Council for Education (England) (London: HMSO, 1963)

A Language for Life [the Bullock Report]. Report of the Committee of Inquiry appointed by the Secretary of State for Education and Science (London: HMSO, 1975)

Teaching Quality [Cmnd. 8836]. Department of Education and Science (London: HMSO, 1983)

Better Schools [Cmnd. 9496]. Department of Education and Science (London: HMSO, 1984)

English from 5 to 16. Curriculum Matters 1. Department of Education and Science (London: HMSO, 1984)

Guidelines for Primary Schools: Language and Literacy. Northern Ireland Council for Educational Development (Belfast: NICED, 1985)

Report of the Committee of Inquiry into the Teaching of English Language [the Kingman Report]. Department of Education and Science (London: HMSO, 1988)

English for asges 5 to 11 [the first Cox Report]. Department of Education and Science (London: DES, 1988)

English for Ages 5 to 16 [the second Cox Report]. Department for Education (London: DFE, 1988)

Proposals for the English Curriculum. Report of the English
Working Group (Belfast: NICC, 1989)

English: Programmes of Study and Attainment Targets. The
Northern Ireland Curriculum (Belfast: HMSO, 1990)

*Key Stages 1 and 2: Programmes of Study and Attainment
Targets.* The Northern Ireland Curriculum (Belfast: HMSO,
1996)

B: Poets' Work:

Auden, W. H.
        The Dyer's Hand (London: Faber, 1963)

Boland, Eavan
        Selected Poems (Manchester, Carcanet, 1989)

Eliot, T. S.
        Collected Poems, 1909-1962 (London: Faber, 1963)
        'That Poetry is Made with Words', *New English
Weekly,* xv, no 2 (27 April 1939)
        *The Waste Land: a Facsimile and Transcript of the
Original Drafts,* edited by Valerie Eliot (London:
Faber, 1971)
        The Sacred Wood: Essays on Poetry and Criticism
(London: Methuen, 1920)
        Selected Essays (London: Faber, 1951)
        'Ulysses, Order and Myth', *The Dial,* lxxv (1923),
480-83

Heaney, Seamus
        Death of a Naturalist (London: Faber, 1966)
        Door into the Dark (London: Faber, 1969)
        Wintering Out (London: Faber, 1972)

North (London: Faber, 1975)
Field Work (London: Faber, 1979)
The Haw Lantern (London: Faber, 1987)
Seeing Things (London: Faber, 1991)
The Spirit Level (London: Faber, 1996)

Preoccupations: Selected Prose 1968 - 1978 (London: Faber, 1980)
An Open Letter (Londonderry: Field Day Theatre, 1983)
The Government of the Tongue (London: Faber, 1988)
The Redress of Poetry: Oxford Lectures (London: Faber, 1995)
'Unhappy and at Home', interview with Seamus Deane, *The Crane Bag,* no 1(1977), 61-67. Reprinted in *The Crane Bag Book of Irish Studies,* 1977-1981 (Dublin: Blackwater Press, 1982), 66-72.
Interview in *The Irish News,* 2 July, 1987
Foreword to *Lifelines: Letters from Famous People about their Favourite Poem,* edited by Niall MacMonagle (Dublin: Tower House, 1992)

Frost, Robert
Selected Poems, edited by Ian Hamilton (Harmondsworth: Penguin, 1973)

Joyce, James
Letters, edited by Richard Ellmann (London: Faber, 1966)

Jones, Peter (ed.)
Imagist Poetry (Harmondsworth: Penguin, 1972)

Longley, Michael
> *Poems 1963-1983* (London: Faber, 1985)

Kavanagh, Patrick
> *Collected Poems* (London: Martin Brian and
O'Keeffe, 1972)

Kennelly, Brendan
> *A Time for Voices: Selected Poems 1960-1990* (New-
castle upon Tyne: Bloodaxe, 1990)
> *The Book of Judas: a Poem* (Newcastle upon Tyne:
Bloodaxe, 1991)
> *Cromwell: a Poem* (Dublin: Beaver Row, 1983)
> *Journey into Joy: Selected Prose,* edited by Ake
Persson (Newcastle upon Tyne: Bloodaxe, 1994)

Larkin, Philip
> *High Windows* (London: Faber, 1974)
> *Collected Poems* (London: Marvell, 1988)
> *Required Writing: Miscellaneous Pieces 1955-1982*
(London: Faber, 1983)

O'Riordan, Sean
> *Brosna* (Dublin: Sairseal and Dill, 1964)

Pound, Ezra
> *Gaudier Brzeska: A Memoir* (London: Bodley Head,
1916)

Yeats, W. B.
> *Collected Poems* (London: Macmillan, 1967)
> *Collected Plays* (London: Macmillan, 1977)
> *Essays and Introductions* (London: Macmillan,
1961)
> *Per Amica Silentia Lunae* (London: Macmillan, 1918)

2: Secondary Sources

Abrams, M. H., *The Mirror and the Lamp: Romantic Theory and the Critical Tradition* (New York: Oxford University Press, 1953)

Allen, David, *English Teaching since 1965: How Much Growth?* (London: Heinemann Educational, 1980)

Beard, Roger, *Children's Writing in the Primary School* (Sevenoaks: Hodder and Stoughton, 1984)

Britton, James, et al., *The Development of Writing Abilities (11-18)* (London: Macmillan, 1975)

Benton, Michael and Geoff Fox, *Teaching Literature: Nine to Fourteen* (Oxford: Oxford University Press, 1985)

Brownjohn, Sandy, *Does It Have to Rhyme? Teaching Children to Write Poetry* (London: Hodder and Stoughton, 1980)
To Rhyme or Not To Rhyme? Teaching Children to Write Poetry (London: Hodder and Stoughton, 1994)

Calkins, Lucy McCormick, *Lessons from a Child: On the Teaching and Learning of Writing* (Exeter, N.H: Heinemann Educational, 1983)

Cox, C. B., *Cox on Cox: An English Curriculum for the 1990s* (London: Hodder and Stoughton, 1991)

Cox, C. B. and A. E. Dyson, *Black Paper [1] Fight for Education* (London: Critical Quarterly Society, 1969)

Cox, C. B. and A. E. Dyson, *Black Paper [2]: The Crisis in Education* (London: Critical Quarterly Society, 1970)

Crystal, David, *The English Language* (London: Penguin, 1988)

　　　　　　Child Language, Linguistics and Learning, 2nd edition (London: Edward Arnold, 1987)

Dixon, John, *Growth through English,* 2nd edition (London: Oxford University Press for the National Association for the Teaching of English, 1967)

Eagleton, Terry, *Literary Theory: An Introduction* (Oxford: Blackwell, 1983)

Graves, Donald H., *Writing: Teachers and Children at Work* (London: Heinemann Educational, 1983)

Hughes, Ted, *Poetry in the Making* (London: Faber, 1967)

Hulme, T. E., *Speculations: Essays on Humanism and the Philosophy of Art,* edited by Herbert Read (London: K. Paul, Trench, Trubner, 1924)

Kermode, Frank, *An Appetite for Poetry: Essays in Literary Interpretation* (London: Collins, 1989)

Langdon, Margaret, *Let the Children Write: An Explanation of Intensive Writing* (London: Longman, 1961)

Leavis, F. R., *English Literature in our Time & the University* (London: Chatto & Windus, 1970)

Lodge, David (ed.), *Modern Criticism and Theory: A Reader* (London: Longman, 1988)

Marsh, George, *Teaching Through Poetry* (London: Hodder and Stoughton, 1988)

Marshall, Sybil, *An Experiment in Education: Writing and the Drafting Process* (London: Cambridge University Press, 1963)

Moffett, James, *Teaching the Universe of Discourse* (Boston: Houghton Mifflin, 1968)

Patterson, Gertrude, *T. S. Eliot: Poems in the Making* (Manchester: Manchester University Press, 1971)
                '"The Waste Land" in the Making', *Critical Quarterly*, 14 (1972), 269-83
                'The Northern Ireland Curriculum for English: a Historical Perspective', in *A Common Curriculum: the Case of Northern Ireland*, edited by Leslie Caul (Belfast: Stranmillis College, 1993), 114-42

Perera, Katherine, *Children's Writing and Reading: Analysing Classroom Language* (Oxford: Blackwell, 1984)

Ricks, Christopher and Leonard Michaels (eds.), *The State of the Language: 1990s edition* (London: Faber, 1990)

Start, K. B., and B. K. Wells, *The Trend of Reading Standards* (Windsor: NFER, 1972)

Steiner, George, *Language and Silence: Essays 1958-1966* (London: Faber, 1967)
                In Bluebeard's Castle: Some Notes Towards the Re-Definition of Culture (London: Faber, 1971)

Stubbs, M., *Discourse Analysis: The Sociolinguistic Analysis of Natural Language* (Oxford: Blackwell, 1983)

Summerfield, Geoffrey, 'Great Expectations', *New Education*, Vol. 2, No. 3, March, 1966

Vygotsky, L. S. *Thought and Language* (Cambridge: Massachusetts Institute of Technology Press, 1962)

Wilkinson, Andrew, et al., *Assessing Language Development* (Oxford: Oxford University Press, 1980)

Wheelwright, Philip, *Metaphor & Reality* (Bloomington: Indiana University Press, 1975)

NOTES ON THE AUTHORS

Gertrude Patterson is head of the English Department at Stranmillis University College Belfast. Author of *T. S. Eliot: Poems in the Making* and a number of other publications on modern poetry, she combines the scholar's knowledge and understanding of poetry together with a teacher's skill in knowing how it should be presented. This new book draws on her research on poetry – the drafting and editing proceses of the poets as shown in their manuscripts – as well as the practical work which she has carried out with teachers, students and pupils from a variety of schools and colleges at primary, secondary and further education levels.

Clare Maloney, a research student of the author, who has contributed a chapter to the publication, is a former teacher from Stabannon, Co. Louth. Now a freelance writer and broadcaster, she is currently engaged in writing materials for the Religious Education curriculum in the Republic of Ireland.